Building 3D Models with modo 701

Learn the art of next generation 3D content creation with step-by-step instructions from a real-world pro

Juan Jiménez García

BIRMINGHAM - MUMBAI

Building 3D Models with modo 701

First published: October 2013

Production Reference: 1181013

Published by Packt Publishing Ltd.
Livery Place
35 Livery Street
Birmingham B3 2PB, UK.

ISBN 978-1-84969-246-5

www.packtpub.com

Cover Image by Juan Jiménez García (contacto@factor3d.com)

Credits

Author
Juan Jiménez García

Reviewers
Oliver Caiden
Martin Kupski
Antonio De Lorenzo
Charles Wardlaw

Acquisition Editors
Anthony Albuquerque
Kartikey Pandey

Lead Technical Editor
Dayan Hyames

Technical Editors
Aparna Chand
Dennis John
Adrian Raposo
Gaurav Thingalaya

Project Coordinator
Angel Jathanna

Proofreaders
Lesley Harrison
Linda Morris

Indexer
Hemangini Bari

Production Coordinator
Nitesh Thakur

Cover Work
Nitesh Thakur

Foreword

Dear readers, starting to work with powerful and complex software of any kind may be a reason for countless moments of frustration. Although modo from Luxology is a modern application with a beautiful and streamlined user interface, the new-user-frustration aspect is not new. If you want to avoid these moments and shorten your learning curve dramatically, then you have come to the right place. Juan Jiménez shares his experience, and will help you to quickly be productive and not waste time fighting the tool. His workflow has been tested and iteratively refined in many real-life projects. Be it cars, furniture, machinery, interior architectural design and visualization, or many other areas, Juan covers a broad range in the computer graphics world. This book is not about theory, it is about how to achieve results, get the job done, and meet deadlines. Only years of experience, intense and passionate use of this great software for a long time, can lead to a book like this. I wish I had access to such a source of inspiration when I started to work with modo. It would have shortened my learning curve a lot as well.

Peter Stammbach,
modo YouTube guru, Switzerland
Peter's YouTube Channel: `http://www.youtube.com/user/stammpe2`

About the Author

Juan Jiménez García started to doodle with 3D software back in 2004, with Lightwave 6. He then started to specialize in modeling, specially hard surface modeling, such as cars, furniture, all kinds of machines and engineering related stuff, and so on. He joined a small broadcasting company in his town, as a camera operator, and in charge of all CG imagery. He also started to explore CG for architectural works. In his spare time, he joined forces with some video game modding groups dedicated to driving simulations, modeling several racing cars for games such as Rfactor and Nascar Racing.

Once he left that company during the middle of 2012, he started to try to make himself visible in the field of interior design, offering visualization services for interior designers. He then opened his own webpage `www.factor3d.com`, and brand named *Factor3D*, which he still develops in the market of CG visualization for several customers in his area, conducting live workshops, and giving private formation with the help of some old work companions, launching a formation center in his town to promote the use of modo.

Many thanks to David, the guy who put a copy of Lightwave in my hands back in the old days and fed my passion for 3D art.

Many thanks to Newtek for developing my beloved Lightwave, which made me learn the basics of 3D imaging.

Many thanks to Brad Peebler and the rest of the guys from Luxology for producing such state of the art piece of software like modo. You guys rock.

Many thanks, finally, to the modo community, who are always giving help to complete strangers willing to learn this awesome software, and for helping me more than I expected, as I now want to help others by writing this humble book.

About the Reviewers

Oliver Caiden is a compositor working at MPC in London.

Martin Kupski is a digital artist who lives in Malmö, Sweden, and was born in 1986. He has worked in the VFX field for several years on everything from small commercials, to big Hollywood productions. He learned the basics at a SOFE (School of Future Entertainment) and honed the skills with the help of tutorials and experience.

Martin has had a lot of different roles, but the skills he has developed the most are Matte painting, compositing, and 3D modeling.

Martin has worked as a freelancer for most of his career. The companies he has worked for include Ghost, Dneg, Postyr, and Gimmick to mention a few. Recently, he has also been teaching the art of Matte painting at Campus i12 in Eksjö. At the time of writing, Martin works at an animation studio called Wilfilm in Copenhagen, as a generalist.

I would like to thank my girlfriend Anna, and my family for their support.

Antonio De Lorenzo is 46 years old and has been working in the CG industry for over 20 years. He is the co-founder of an Italian company called the *Imago Edizioni*, with his brother Francesco De Lorenzo. They publish magazines, books, and lead as editors, a CGI portal (`www.imaginaction.com`), with forums for the 2D and 3D graphics community in Italy. He has translated four books about ZBrush, and other three for 3DS Max from English, and other graphics packages. He teaches CGI to universities and private schools, and works as a school manager, supervisor, and coordinator for some 3D courses, and as a teacher for single 3D matter too.

Imago Edizioni makes the production betatester for a lot of worldwide 3D packages, and is active in 3D production, including still images and animations for various 3D visualization fields, from Medicine to TV, from Architecture to Jewel Design and Digital Nature.

Charles Wardlaw is a Character Technical Director for film and television, including work on *Resident Evil: Retribution*, *Mama*, and *The Mortal Instruments: City of Bones*. He uses Python and C++ for creating custom rigging solutions to solve problems and facilitate animator workflows, and enjoys the challenges present in each new script. In his off hours he enjoys photography, watches cartoons from the 80's, attempts to draw, maintains the tradigiTOOLS animation plugin for Maya, for FUNhouse Interactive, and teaches his daughter how to box.

I'd like to thank my wife for being the most amazing and supportive woman I've ever met.

www.PacktPub.com

Support files, eBooks, discount offers and more

You might want to visit www.PacktPub.com for support files and downloads related to your book.

Did you know that Packt offers eBook versions of every book published, with PDF and ePub files available? You can upgrade to the eBook version at www.PacktPub.com and as a print book customer, you are entitled to a discount on the eBook copy. Get in touch with us at service@packtpub.com for more details.

At www.PacktPub.com, you can also read a collection of free technical articles, sign up for a range of free newsletters and receive exclusive discounts and offers on Packt books and eBooks.

http://PacktLib.PacktPub.com

Do you need instant solutions to your IT questions? PacktLib is Packt's online digital book library. Here, you can access, read and search across Packt's entire library of books.

Why Subscribe?

- Fully searchable across every book published by Packt
- Copy and paste, print and bookmark content
- On demand and accessible via web browser

Free Access for Packt account holders

If you have an account with Packt at www.PacktPub.com, you can use this to access PacktLib today and view nine entirely free books. Simply use your login credentials for immediate access.

Table of Contents

Preface

There are always a lot of people asking me very basic questions about my work in 3D art.

Sadly, learning how to use 3D software can be tedious and difficult, especially if you base your advances in self learning, which can imply double the effort. This book will focus on those kind of people who want to grow their skills in Luxology modo, but find the information about this software sometimes too hard to find or too technical for a beginner.

As that was the case when I started developing my skills in 3D art, I want to help others to understand the basics of this great piece of software, as I wanted to have in my early days. So, what you will find here is less technical information, and more practical definitions and examples, straight to the point and without unnecessary and confusing terminology.

I hope you all enjoy this book the same way as I enjoyed, writing it for you.

What this book covers

Chapter 1, Knowing the Interface, introduces the general use of the software's interface.

Chapter 2, Beginning with Modeling, will teach the use of the modeling tools.

Chapter 3, Texturing and Materials, covers the use of textures and materials as we see them in the real world.

Chapter 4, Illuminating a Scene, explains the use of different types of lights and illumination techniques.

Chapter 5, Preparing a Shot, covers many good practices to be carried out at the time of taking a picture of your scene.

Chapter 6, Rendering your Scene, will teach you how to set up your scene to get the best results.

Chapter 7, The Post-production Phase, covers a great number of methods to enhance your final render.

What you need for this book

You will need the following for the book:

- Luxology modo 701
- Adobe Photoshop CS3 or higher

Who this book is for

People looking for an introduction to the world of 3D art, newcomers, or those with a little knowledge of using 3D software in general, or Luxology modo in particular.

Conventions

In this book, you will find a number of styles of text that distinguish between different kinds of information. Here are some examples of these styles, and an explanation of their meaning.

Code words in text are shown as follows: '"I renamed mine to `depth`.'"

New terms and **important words** are shown in bold. Words that you see on the screen, in menus or dialog boxes for example, appear in the text like this: '"and a third button called **RAY GL**, which is off by default'".

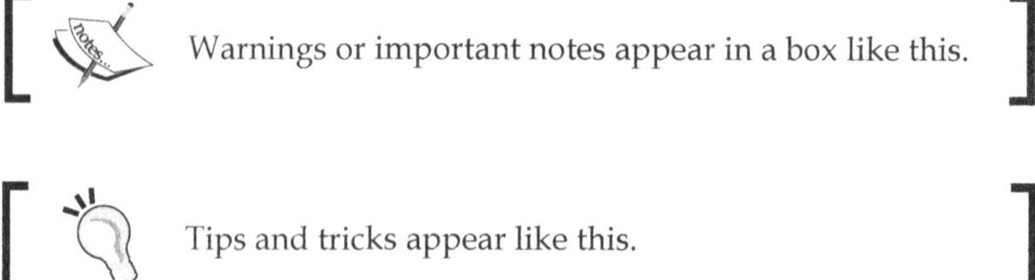

Warnings or important notes appear in a box like this.

Tips and tricks appear like this.

Reader feedback

Feedback from our readers is always welcome. Let us know what you think about this book—what you liked or may have disliked. Reader feedback is important for us to develop titles that you really get the most out of.

To send us general feedback, simply send an e-mail to `feedback@packtpub.com`, and mention the book title via the subject of your message. If there is a topic that you have expertise in and you are interested in either writing or contributing to a book, see our author guide on `www.packtpub.com/authors`.

Customer support

Now that you are the proud owner of a Packt book, we have a number of things to help you to get the most from your purchase.

Downloading the images of this book

We also provide you a PDF file that has the images of the screenshots/diagrams used in this book. The images will help you better understand the changes in the output. You can download this file from `http://www.packtpub.com/sites/default/files/downloads/2465OT_Graphics_Bundle.pdf`

Errata

Although we have taken every care to ensure the accuracy of our content, mistakes do happen. If you find a mistake in one of our books—maybe a mistake in the text or the code—we would be grateful if you would report this to us. By doing so, you can save other readers from frustration and help us improve subsequent versions of this book. If you find any errata, please report them by visiting `http://www.packtpub.com/submit-errata`, selecting your book, clicking on the **errata submission form** link, and entering the details of your errata. Once your errata are verified, your submission will be accepted and the errata will be uploaded on our website, or added to any list of existing errata, under the Errata section of that title. Any existing errata can be viewed by selecting your title from `http://www.packtpub.com/support`.

Piracy

Piracy of copyright material on the Internet is an ongoing problem across all media. At Packt, we take the protection of our copyright and licenses very seriously. If you come across any illegal copies of our works, in any form, on the Internet, please provide us with the location address or website name immediately so that we can pursue a remedy.

Please contact us at `copyright@packtpub.com` with a link to the suspected pirated material.

We appreciate your help in protecting our authors, and our ability to bring you valuable content.

Questions

You can contact us at `questions@packtpub.com` if you are having a problem with any aspect of the book, and we will do our best to address it.

1

Knowing the Interface

Before we put our hands on the software, let's spend a few minutes learning how modo is organized so that we can use its features wisely. Learning how modo works as a whole can help us optimize our workflow. So, double-click on your modo shortcut and let's see what's in there.

In this chapter, we will cover the following aspects:

- Using the viewports
- Working with tabs
- Understanding the tools panel
- Understanding the info panel
- Working with the selection methods

Using viewports

If you have some previous experience with 3D software, you will notice a typical 3D interface and a big workspace showing a single perspective view surrounded by a bunch of buttons. If you are new to all this, then it's time to explain what this is all about.

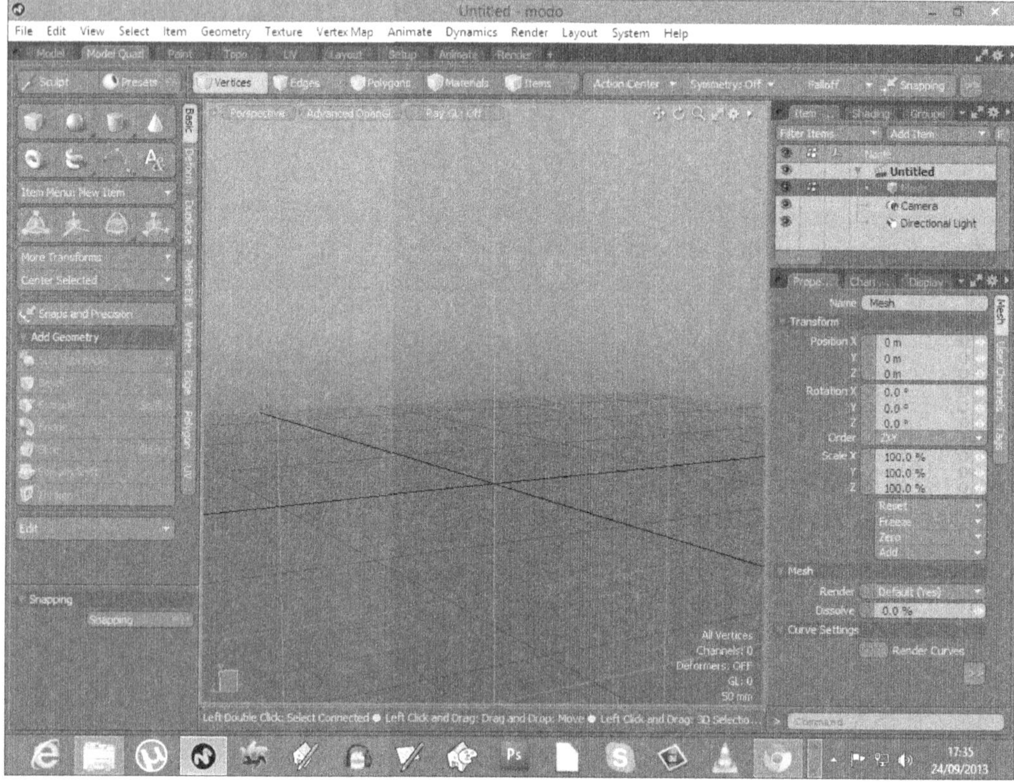

First of all, take a look at what will be the main workspace you will be using. A single perspective visor occupies the main part of the screen. That's a perspective view of your model. If you look at the top of it, you will see the information you need to identify it.

This information is divided in to two parts: information about the visor and how it displays the view (in the left-hand side corner), and general controls for zooming, panning, and rotating the basic stuff. You can see three big buttons in the left corner of each visor (giving information about the view represented, the kind of display it is showing, and a third button called **RAY GL**, which is off by default). We will see the RAY GL mode later on, since it's related to the rendering phase, but it's important to know about the other two.

For the first button, you will notice there is a difference in each viewport. I'm sure you have guessed the meaning of it. It's telling you what view you are seeing in each one. That's **Top** for the top view, **Perspective** for the perspective view, and so on. We will see their uses in the customizing part.

These viewports (and the layout of viewports) are customizable, as we will see later. But for now, just know that you have all the information for the visual control of your scene.

Controlling the viewports

Let's focus on controlling the viewports. Viewports are not fixed in any way. You can manipulate them, change their size, position, maximize/minimize them, change their properties, and so on. That's what the control area—on the top-right of each visor—is for. Since this section will talk about controlling the viewport, we will cover the use of the top-right controls.

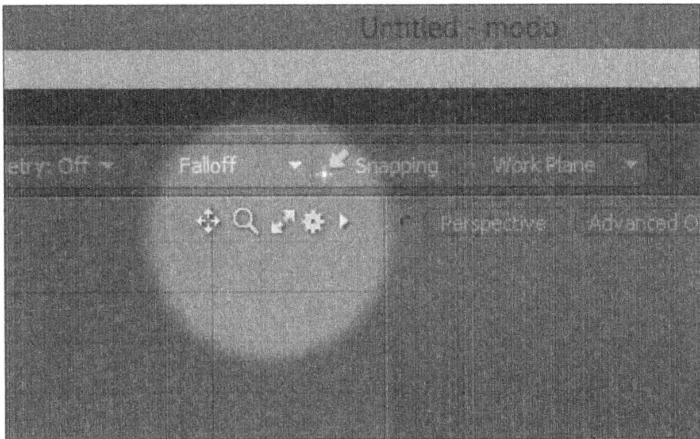

If you look at the previous screenshot, there are a number of icons, some of them very clear about their function and others not. Let me explain what each of them do:

The panning tool

The first icon is for panning. You can click-and-drag this icon to pan over the image.

The rotating tool

The second is for rotating. Click-and-drag over this icon to rotate the image. Of course, this button only works in a perspective or camera visor, since the rest of the views are unable to rotate, due to its very nature.

The zooming tool

The third is the zooming control. Again, click-and-drag left or right to zoom in and out.

The maximizing tool

The fourth is the maximize button. Nothing fancy here. Just click on it and the visor will expand to occupy the whole workspace. Click on it again to return to the previous viewport setup.

The options button

The fifth (the one shaped as a gear) is the options button. If you click on it, a menu will show up with all the options you need to customize that particular visor. It's divided into tabs, each one related to particular aspects of the visor. You can change things such as visibility of the wireframe, colors, mesh displays, and backgrounds. But for now, and being an introductory explanation of the interface, my advice is that you don't mess too much with this menu. The standard values should be good for you. Anyway, feel free (and it's a good thing) to experiment with some of these options to see the effect on the display of the viewport.

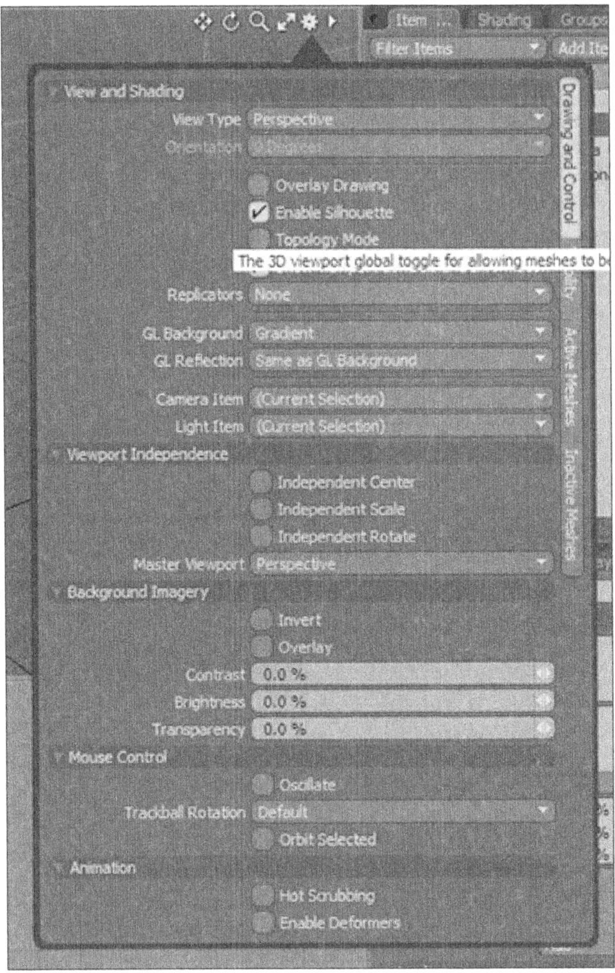

Customizing the viewport quad

Now that we know how to control the views, we can move on to the next step, which will be customizing the viewports as per our own likings.

For this, we will look at the top-left corner of any viewport. You will see a set of three buttons. As I said earlier, we will ignore the third button (**RAY GL**) and will instead focus on the other two.

If you look at the preceding screenshot, you will see the first button says **Perspective**. As you guessed, this button shows us information about the type of view that visor is showing. Notice that there is a different view on each of the viewports. Of course, you can change the view to the one you like. Click on that first button to see a menu of views you can switch to. There are options to change the view to the camera view or to the light view.

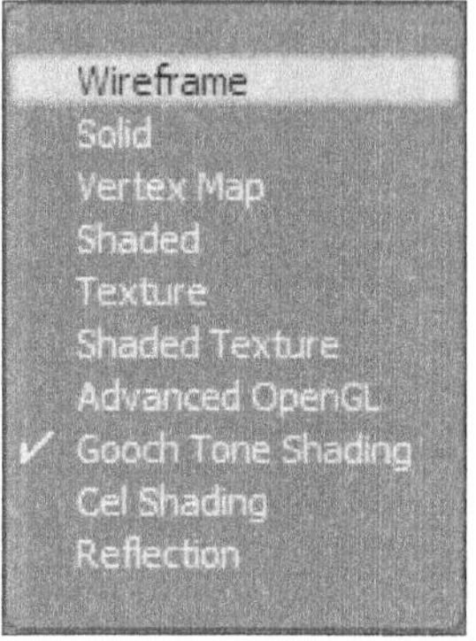

The second button is a bit more complex. It tells us the style of view this viewport is giving. In the preceding screenshot, you will see the list of styles you can choose. There are many, and as each have their own strong points, you will choose the one that is more useful for you depending on what you are doing.

Personally, the most important styles for me are wireframe, advanced OpenGL, and reflection. For me, these three styles are the basic styles you will be using most of the time. Let me show the difference between them briefly with the following screenshot:

In the preceding screenshot, you can see the three styles side-by-side; first is the wireframe. This style lets us see what's not visible normally (the back of the model or hidden parts). It also shows us a clear understanding of the topology of the mesh.

The second style is called **Advanced Open GL**. It shows models with textures applied. It's useful to see our model with correctly-scaled textures applied. It also shows basic reflections in real time. This is very useful if we want to see a fast preview of our texturing, especially if we disable the wireframe in the options menu of the viewport, which is a good practice for new users to get used to from the beginning.

The third image is the reflection style. What this style shows is how the reflections will be calculated in that mesh (if we set its material to be reflective). This is very useful to see (even if the material is not reflective) how the mesh "flows", that is, if the modeling is well organized. So, if you rotate the visor in the reflection mode, you will see in real time how the reflections flow all across the model. If there is any bad modeling, the reflections will tell you. Look at the following screenshot to see the ugly reflections from a bad modeling:

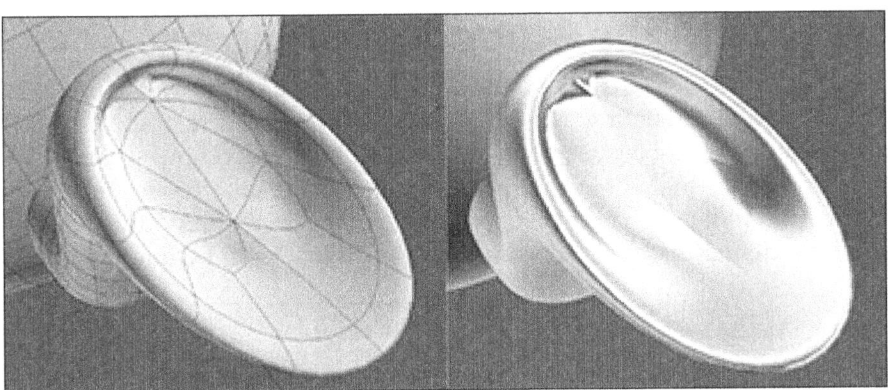

As a last tip, you can also redistribute the viewports in the workspace. If you look at the interface, you will see that the visors are framed. And you can use the frames to resize the visors. That's simple! Just drag the vertical frame to the left or the right of the screen and you will see how one of the sides becomes bigger while the other becomes smaller. Drag the horizontal frame and the same will occur, but with the top and bottom part of the screen. You can also drag all the frames at once by dragging the point where the two frames meet (the center of the screen) and moving it freely while all the visors are resized according to where you drag their center.

Working with tabs

modo's interface is divided into different workspaces, each one contained in a tab. You can see the tabs displayed at the top of the interface. Each of the tabs refers to different kinds of things you can do with modo in a themed interface. For example, in the **Animate** tab, you will find all the tools and panels you will need for animating things. The same goes for every other tab, so depending on what phase of the production you are at, you will by using at least one of these tabs. Let's take a look at the two basic tabs we will be using through out this book: Model and Render. As this book is for beginners, we will only be dealing with the **Model** and **Render** tabs in future chapters. The rest of the tabs cover more advanced tasks such as UV mapping, character rigging, and texture painting.

Working with the Model Quad tab

Under this tab, you will find all the tools available for the modeling phase. In fact, there are two tabs for modeling: **Model** and **Model Quad**. We're going to use the **Model Quad** tab just because it gives us more information (and we can still maximize the visor to make it look like the regular Model tab). Notice the only difference between the two is the visor workspace, where there is only one big visor in the **Model** tab and a standard quad visor in the **Model Quad** tab.

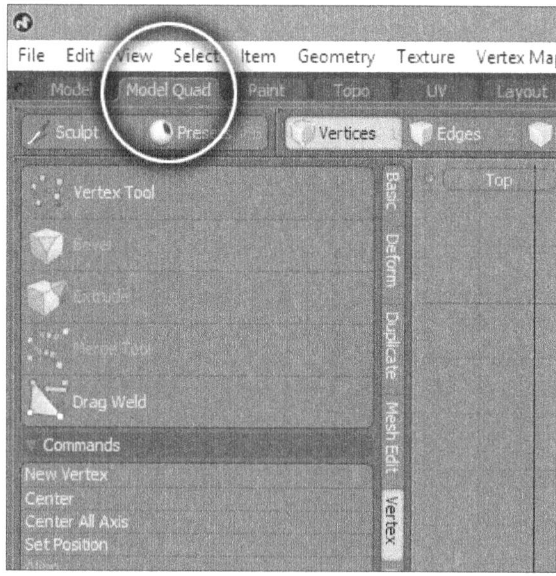

This layout is divided into three main spaces:

- **Tools panel**: Here you can choose all the different tools to generate geometry, modify it, and so on. It is also divided into tabs (vertical tabs in this case). Don't be impressed by this "tabs-into-tabs" thing. You will notice later that this is a very practical approach to help your workflow.
- **Visors quad**: This is self-explanatory. This is the main workspace with four customizable visors. This is where you will be doing things most of the time.
- **Properties panel**: This is divided into tabs as the Tools panel is, but this one gives you information about organizing the scene. Depending on what tab you are using, you will be controlling the different layers of the scene or the materials, lights, settings, and so on.

Working with the Render tab

Under the **Render** tab, you will see a slightly different layout aimed to work better in the rendering phase, as shown in the following screenshot:

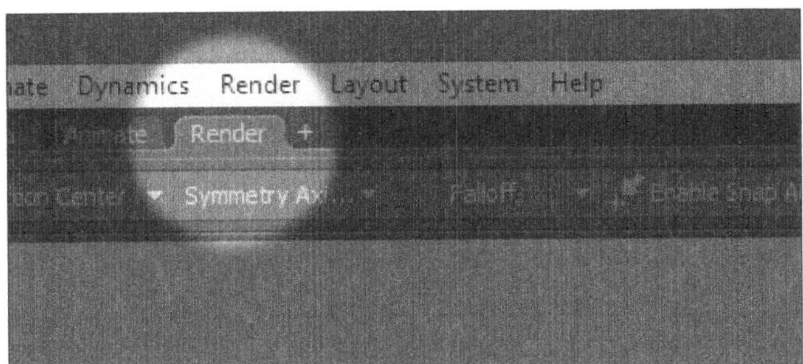

It's basically divided into three columns, showing the following:

- **Two viewports**: The upper viewport is for the preview render and the bottom one to use it as a working viewport. This bottom viewport has tabs to access additional useful editors.
- **Two panels**: The upper panel is for controlling the items of the scene and the bottom one to work with the materials.
- **Properties panel**: This is where you can control the details about the things you choose in the middle column.

Understanding the Tools panel

Now that we get the idea that modo's interface is divided into tabs, we're going to take a more in-depth look at what's under each one. Starting with the **Model Quad** tab, I want you to check the top-left panel, named the **Tools** panel. It contains the modeling tools you will need. Using these tools, we will be able to generate geometry, modify it, and make all sorts of operations in order to get our modeling done. Let's look at this panel in detail:

Using the Basic tab

The **Basic** tab contains the basic operations for modeling. From here, you can generate primitives, manipulate your model (move, rotate, and scale), and perform other procedures that we will see later in this chapter.

So, what is a primitive? A primitive is a basic starting point from which you can build more complex models. These kind of objects are extremely basic (cubes, spheres, and the like). You can see what type of primitive you can generate just by taking a look at the buttons on the panel. You click on the **Cube** button, and you draw a cube; simple. There are two ways to generate a primitive:

- **By using the corresponding tool**: Let's say you want to create a cube. The task is simple: just click on the **Cube** button and start drawing the cube inside any of the visors. First draw the base and then give it some height using the controllers.
- **Generating a unit primitive**: If you press *Ctrl* and click on any of the primitives buttons, you will create a unit primitive. It's a simple shortcut to make primitive generation more simple and quick. By using this method, a standard primitive will be automatically generated without the need to draw anything.

Which method you choose for primitive creation will depend on your own preferences and the task at hand. It can often be more practical to generate a unit primitive and then modify it instead of using the tools to create a primitive of a specified size.

Using the Vertex/Edge/Polygon tabs

A mesh is formed by vertices, edges, and polygons. Their corresponding tabs will give you the tools to deal with each element. These three tabs are essential to work in the different selection modes (we will discuss this later). Let's take a look at what's basic about each one.

The Vertex tab

Under this tab, you will find many tools and operations related to vertexes:

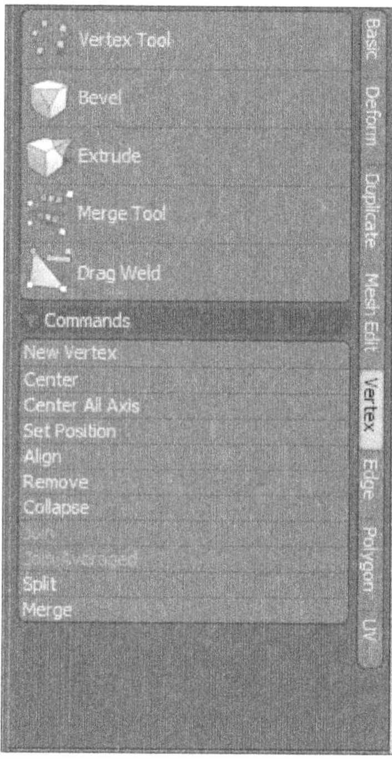

Let me show you the main and more practical options you will find here:

- **Center/Center All Axis**: An axis is the imaginary line used as a reference for any of the dimensions in a 3D universe. Typically, axes are named x, y, and z (for width, height, and depth). I use this option very often. What it does is it takes all the selected vertices and places them in the center of every axis, which is the same as saying the center of the scene. This is very useful when I want to center a whole model. Just switch to vertex mode, click on **Center All Axis**, and the whole scene will be correctly placed in the exact center. If you use **Center** instead, a pop-up dialog will ask you for the axis you want your selection to be centered on. You choose which one is better for you at any given moment.
- **Join**: This option joins two or more vertices to form a single one. The resulting vertex will be placed exactly in the same place as the last vertex selected, so the formula will be something like "join a to b".
- **Join average**: This is the same as Join, but the result will be a single vertex placed in the middle of the selection. It is useful for joining offset vertices.

- **Merge**: This option scans the mesh looking for overlapping vertices (two or more vertices overlapping each other) and then merges them into a single vertex. It is good for cleaning your models or to automatically weld parts of the model. You can set a threshold level so only certain distances between vertices get merged.

The preceding screenshot shows how the merge distance setting can affect the mesh. From left to right, as the distance value increases, the welding pairs of points become farther from each other. Normally, the default value works well, but in case you have troubles with the tool skipping some areas, you can try to fix it by increasing the threshold, thus forcing problematic areas to be welded.

The Edge tab

Manipulating the edges of a model is always a very powerful way to work. From this tab, you will find many useful tools that will make your life easier.

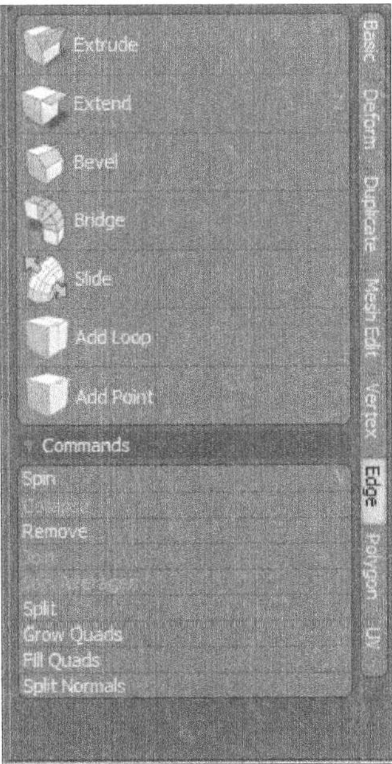

The ones I like the most are as follows:

- **Extend**: Select an edge and click on this tool. Now, using the on-screen controls, you can control a newly generated polygon born from the selected edge. It is very useful if you want to grow your mesh from basic to complex shapes.

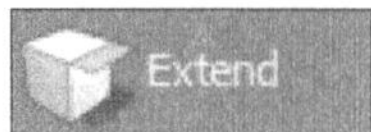

- **Bevel**: Select an edge (or a group of edges) and make them round with this tool. You can control the roundness of the beveling with the tool's properties to give it more or less definition. This is extremely handy if you want to add details to your model or generate new geometry in a existing mesh.

- **Bridge**: This generates a polygon connecting two edges. You select the two edges (or a group of edges), click on the tool, and they will be bridged. You can also control how the bridge works, if you want it segmented.

- **Slide**: Select one or more edges and move them with this tool without the need to adjust the shape of the mesh. The mesh will be dynamically updated while you drag the edges. This is a great tool for making fine adjustments to your model.

- **Add loop/Loop slice**: These two tools are used to add geometry based on an edge or a group of edges. You click on **Add Loop** and then click on an edge on the visor. It will add a cut generating the geometry. Another way is using the loop slice tool, which is more flexible and versatile to my taste. You can find the tool in the upper menu by navigating to **Geometry** | **Slice** | **Loop**.

- **Remove**: The best way to get rid of one or more edges is just by using the **Remove** button. Select the edge you want to remove and click on the tool. The edge will disappear, but preserving the mesh involved. It's different than selecting the edge and hitting the backspace key, since this last method is destructive (it removes not only the edge, but all the geometry that edge was forming part of) while the remove method is non-destructive.

The Polygon tab

You will be using this tab most of the time. It equals—if not overcomes—the **Edge** tab in terms of usefulness:

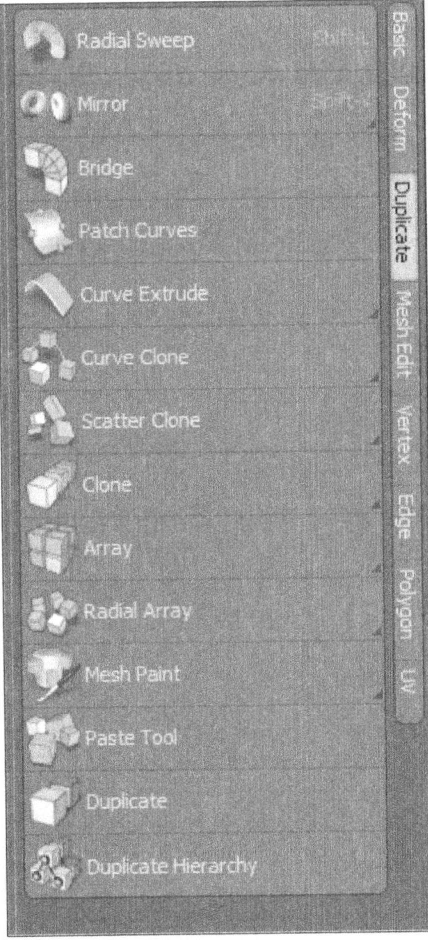

Once again, we will not look at the full range of tools here, but we will focus on the most useful tools and the tools you will find most useful when you first start modeling:

- **Bevel**: Similar to beveling an edge, you can bevel a polygon. The **Bevel** tool creates a new polygon, making an inset (scaling down the polygon to its own center) of the original one combined with a shift (extruding it along its face orientation). Both inset and shift can be positive or negative depending on whether the inset/shift is applied to the outside or the inside of the polygon. It is very useful for making things such as tips of poles, modeling frames, and making holes.

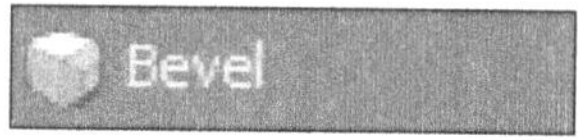

- **Smooth shift**: This one is similar to the **Bevel** tool. The difference is that when dealing with curvy shapes, smooth shift seems to handle it better. My advice is that you use both tools and decide which one you like more. Personally, I prefer the simplicity of the **Bevel** tool, but again, it's your choice.

- **Bridge**: This is the same exact thing as bridging edges, but applied to polygons.

- **Flip**: In the 3D world, polygons aren't like a sheet of paper where you have a front face and a back face. Polygons are single-sided by default, so if you look at a polygon from behind, it will become invisible. The property that defines which face is visible is called **normal**. It basically states the direction the polygon is looking, leaving its back invisible. This tool actually flips the normal of the selected polygon.

Use this tool to make a polygon face one side or the other. This might sound silly, but it's useful when you are modeling and you find the geometry is being generated for some reason facing the wrong direction. Another good use is when you model a room and you use the **Flip** tool to make the floor, cellar, and walls face inside. So, when you see the model from the outside, the walls are invisible, but they get visible if you place the camera inside making it possible to have the walls not blocking the camera view.

In the previous screenshot, each polygon is facing a different direction. So, we must say its normals are opposite. The left polygon is facing the camera while the right polygon is facing the opposite direction.

- **Set Material**: This is an essential tool, of course, when you want to assign a material to some selected polygons. You will be using it all the time in its corresponding phase (materials and texturing).

Set Material

Using the Duplicate tab

When dealing with modeling operations involving copying a mesh—or part of it—we will use the tools from the **Duplicate** tab:

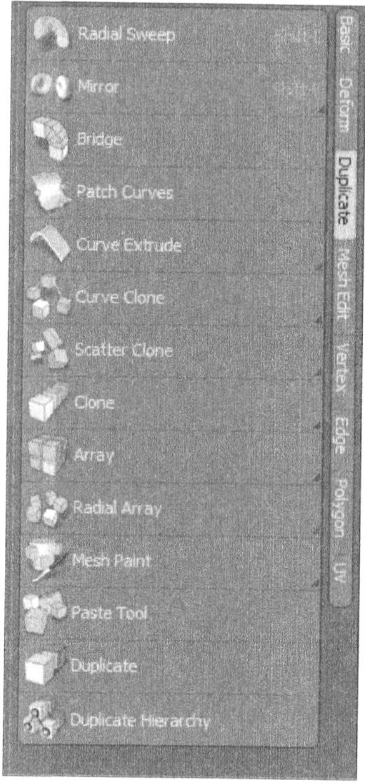

The **Duplicate** tab is where you find the tools for everything related to making copies of the geometry or even the entire model. There are several tools here, and they are all more or less a bit advanced. Following the approach of the book, we will look at the main duplicate operations we will be using to get started with modeling. Let's check them out:

- **Mirror**: This is classic mirror operation. This means that you will duplicate the selected object or geometry selection according to the tool's properties. A common operation is to make a symmetry, for example, modeling only one side of a face, then mirroring it to generate the other side.

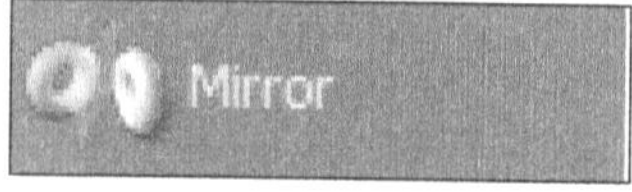

- **Clone**: This is a very handy tool to create copies of an object easily. With it, you can generate a number of copies without the need of making a manual copy/paste operation several times, thus saving you time. You can, for example, model an entire fence just by creating a single stake and making a bunch of copies in a single click. You can also use an offset value to modify the clones so that each one will be moved by the previous amount plus the offset.

- **Array**: This is something like an advanced clone tool. It follows the same principles as cloning but you get more control. In addition to cloning an object, you can set the axes you want to clone through, apply an offset, and so on. Imagine yourself modeling a restaurant hall. Of course you will not be modeling each table and every set of chairs. You will not even clone it a number of times. You will want to use the Array tool, modeling one single set and then cloning it in an array of, let's say, 5 x 5 elements and you're done.

- **Radial Array**: The same goes for the Radial Array tool, the only difference is that you don't work with the axis to establish the cloning, but with an angle number that defines how much degrees of a full 360° turn will cover the cloning. If you want to model the spokes of a bike, this is your tool.

Using the Mesh Edit tab

The **Mesh Edit** tab is an all-purpose tab for modifying your model. It contains various interesting tools that you can use—and you will use—very often, regardless of being in vertex, edge, or polygon mode:

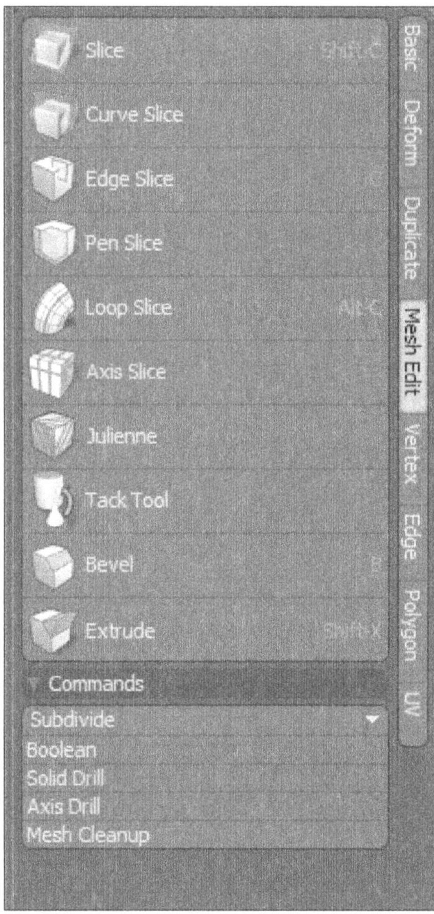

Most of my work is based around these tools. Let me show you the most used tools you will find here:

- **Edge Slice**: This tool lets us draw cuts throughout the mesh as if we were using a cutting knife. You can go placing points anywhere on the surface of the mesh and they will connect themselves, creating more geometry.

- **Pen Slice**: This one is a variation of the **Edge Slice** tool. You must be working in one of the orthographic views (top, right, left, and so on) and it will let you draw freely without having to take edges, polygons, or vertices. Once the slices are done, you can switch to a perspective view to find that your slices are in fact projected to the geometry of the mesh.

- **Loop Slice**: Maybe the tool I use most. With this tool, you can add a slice to an entire loop in a single click. What makes this tool so powerful is that you can use it on edges or polygons or change the behavior of it if you want to change how the slices are created. We will discuss this later in more depth.

- **Extrude**: The extrude tool is a timeless classic in every 3D software. An extrusion is when you create a new polygon from an existing one by shifting the new geometry out along a defined vector. Imagine a skyscraper rising from the underground.

The following figure shows a clear example of what an extrusion is:

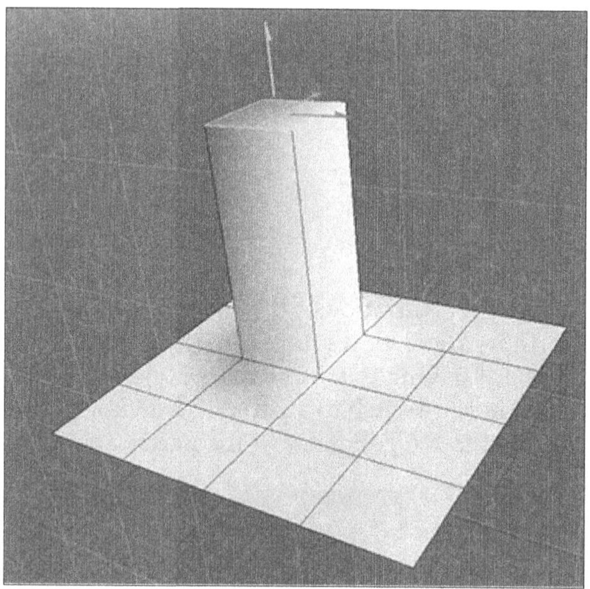

- **Boolean**: The **Boolean** tool is a very classic operation too. This tool lets you merge two different objects, forming a single mesh. The intersecting geometry is removed and a new joining geometry is created. This option has got many settings, mainly affecting its behavior, so you can make a subtraction Boolean, Intersect Boolean, adding Boolean, and so on.

In the following figure, you can see examples of the main three Boolean operations. From left to right, they are as follows: **Subtract**, **Intersect**, and **Add**:

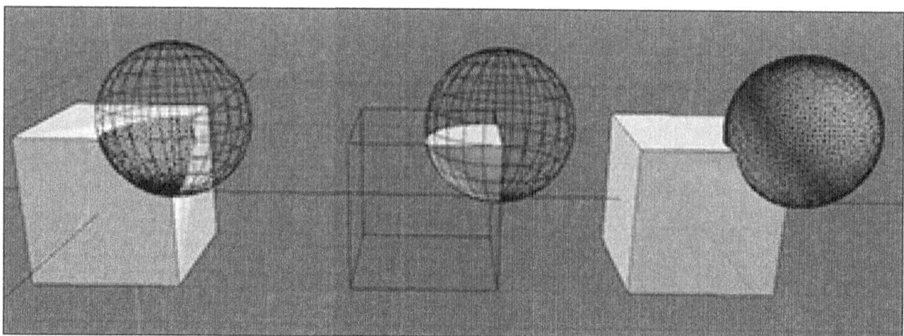

To perform a Boolean operation, you need two objects, each one in a separate layer. Select the object you want to be affected from the items list. Activate the tool and choose the Boolean mode you want for it. When you click on **OK**, the action will be performed and you will get the corresponding result.

Understanding the Info panel

The right part of the screen will always be occupied by the **Info** panel. It shows a general view of the organization of the scene:

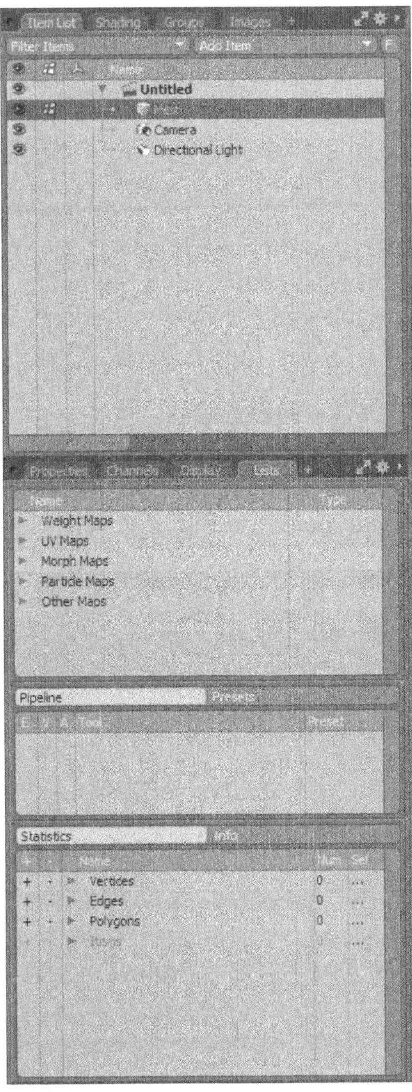

Located in the top section, it contains two of the most important panels in modo: the items list and the shader tree.

Using the Item List panel

The **Item List** panel is the panel that will show you general information about the scene. It contains the list of layers that make up the scene as well as other basic items.

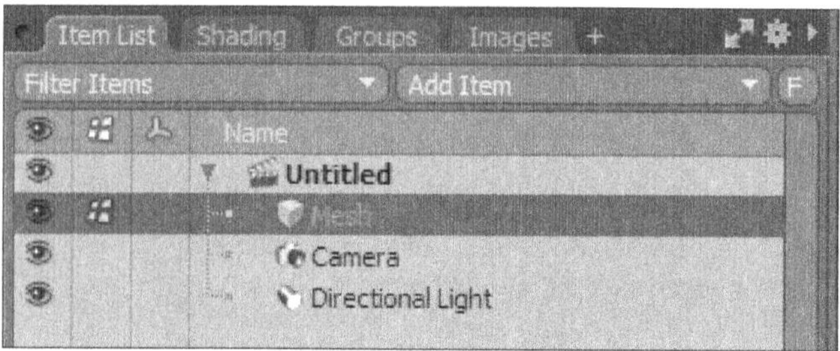

By default, in a newly created scene, it contains only one layer, a camera item, and a light item (a **Directional Light** by default). For a reference, you should have in mind that **mesh layers** in modo are the same as objects in most 3D packages.

Using the Shading panel

The **Shading** panel is essential during the material/texturing phase. It contains in-depth information about the various shaders we will be using, the list of materials created, the render settings, and many more things that we will discuss later.

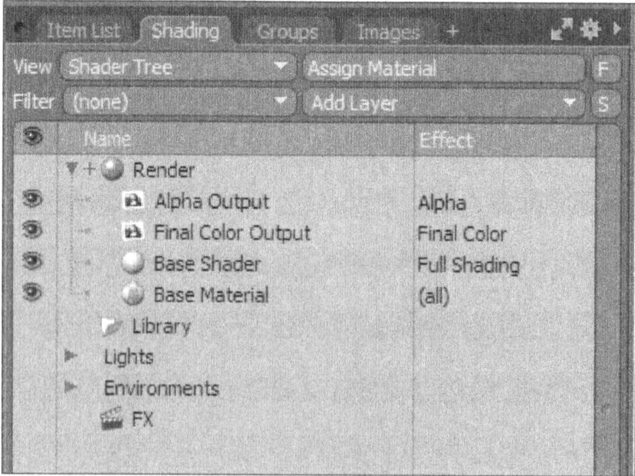

Using the Properties panel

Located right under the **Shading** panel, we see the **Properties** panel. This is a dynamic panel that will show us information about whatever we have selected in the items list or the shading tree.

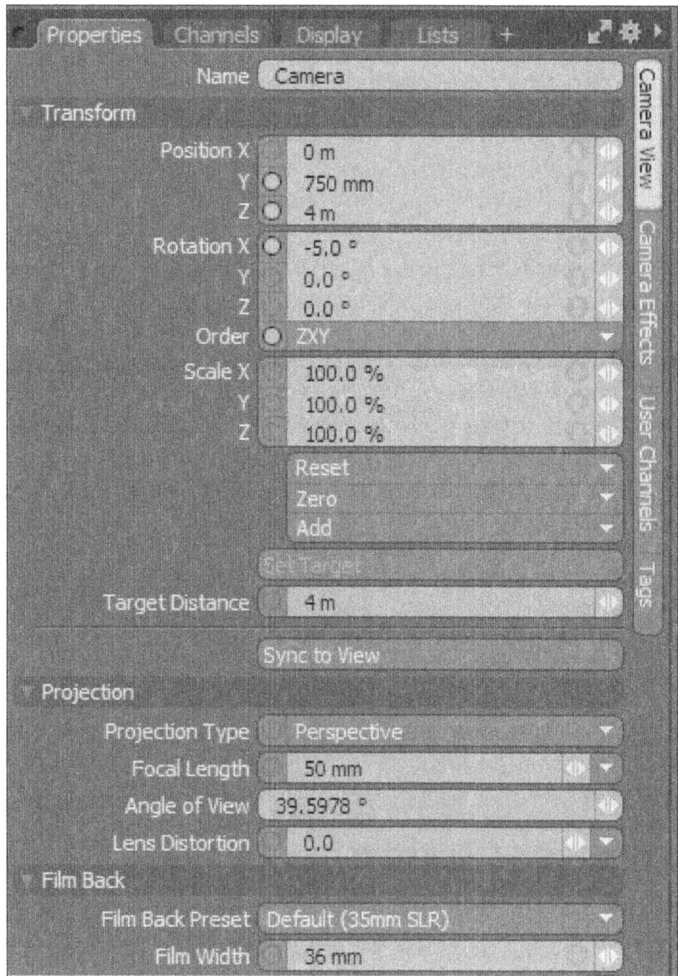

If you have your camera selected, it will show information about the camera's properties. It will do the same if you have a material selected, a shader, and so on.

Working with selection methods

It might sound silly, but selecting and deselecting things is a task that we will be carrying out most of the time, so a solid and agile method of selection is a must if we want a fluid pipeline. Here I will show the basic and most practical selection methods in modo.

The polygon/vertex/edge modes

Look at your cursor. By default, it will show a custom shape in modo, showing a crosshair with two dots. Now press the spacebar key. The cursor changes its shape to a crosshair with a diagonal line. If you don't see a crosshair with two dots, make sure you're in the vertex mode by pressing *1* on the keyboard. Press the spacebar key one more time. Now the cursor is the same crosshair, but with a little square right next to it. What does it mean?

If you look at the top of the interface, you will see a toolbar as in the previous figure. Those five buttons change between selection modes. Depending on the selection mode you are working on, it will highlight to show you what mode you are in. We will focus on the first three modes (**Vertices**, **Edges**, and **Polygons**). You can click on them to change modes, but an easy shortcut is simply hitting the space key, as you just did, to cycle through them.

Needless to say, you will be working on different parts of the model depending on your selection mode. If you are in the **Edges** mode, you can only select and work on edges. The same goes for the vertex mode and the polygons mode.

Making quick selections

Modo has got very useful and quick methods to make selections. These selection methods can be found in the top menu under **Select**. I will show the main quick selection methods I use:

- **Select connected polys**: In the case you want to quickly select an entire mesh, the best and quicker solution is, in polygon selection mode, to double-click on a polygon. The selection will expand to every polygon connected to the first. In a practical sense, you double-click on a poly and the entire object gets selected.

- **Select loop of polys**: There will be times when you need to select a loop of polys. To do that quickly, just select two adjacent polys in the loop and press *L*. The corresponding loop of polys gets selected automatically.
- **Select loop of edges**: This is the same procedure as for selecting connected polys. If you want to select an entire loop of edges, just double-click on one of the edges and the corresponding loop will be selected.
- **Edge ring selection**: Similar to the select loop, but mainly applied to edges. When you select an edge (or a group of edges), by pressing *Alt* + *L*, all the parallel edges placed into the original loops of polys containing the edge will be selected. You can see it clearly in the following figure:

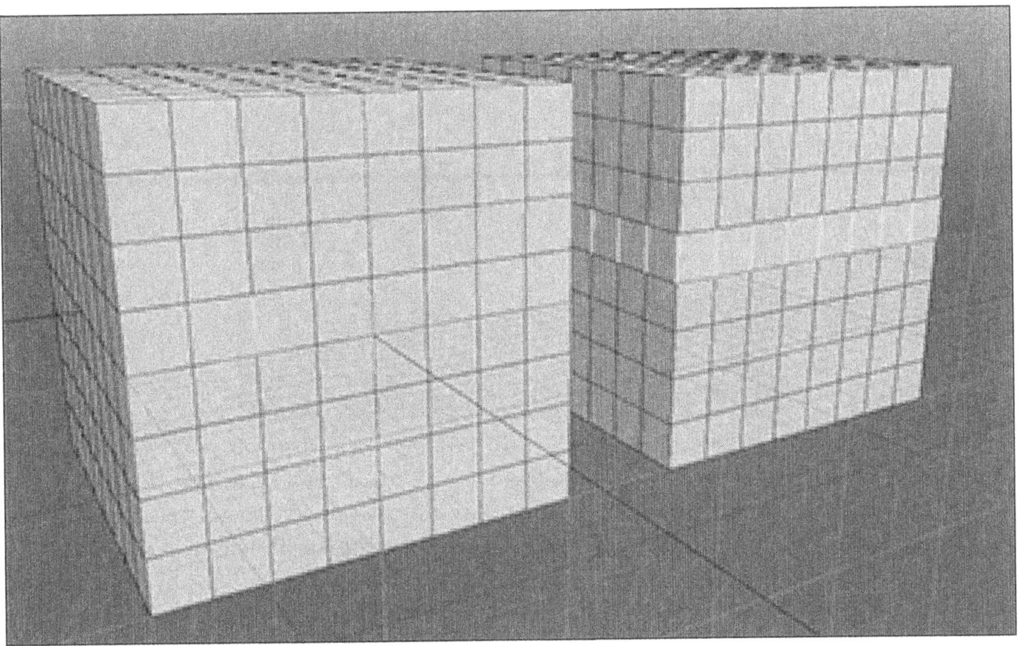

As you can see, if we first select an edge and make a ring selection, all the parallel edges of the same loop will be selected.

Using the Lasso selection tool

If you right-click and drag in the visor, you can draw a free-hand selection. When you release the mouse, everything inside that shape will be selected. This is what we call a lasso selection. It's a quick way to make selections manually:

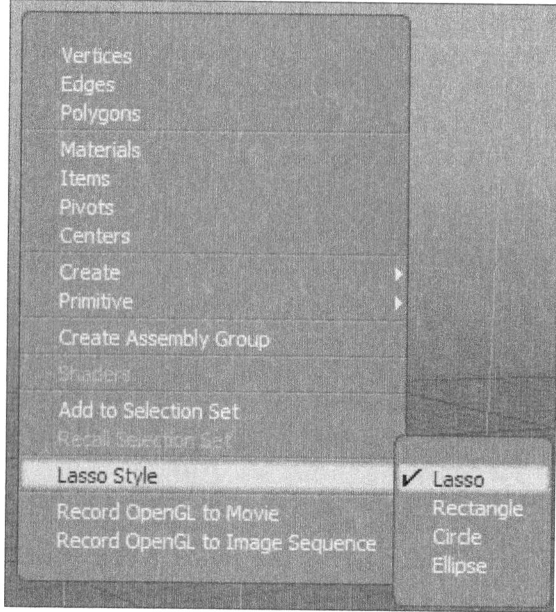

There will be cases when the lasso selection won't be the best approach to make a selection. You may want to select a square area or a circular one. In these cases, you will want to work with a different selection style than the lasso. Right-click on an empty area of the visor; a pop-up menu will appear. If you look at the bottom part of the menu, you will find an option called **Lasso Style**. This option lets us change the style of the lasso to other shapes: **Rectangle**, **Circle**, and **Ellipse**.

Hiding and unhiding

Isolating a selection can be a good idea when you have a very complex model and you want to focus on a specific part. You can do that in many ways, but for me, the best option is using the hide/unhide tool.

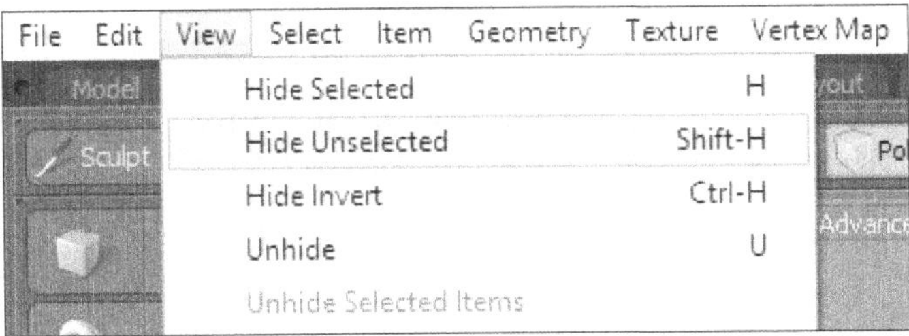

It is located under **View** in the upper menu. It's options are the following:

- **Hide selected**: In case you want to make something disappear, just select it and use this option.
- **Hide unselected**: This is the opposite case. If you want to isolate your selection, use this option, and the rest of the model will disappear.
- **Hide invert**: You can use this option to switch the visibility between what is selected and what is not. This means that if you have a selection created and you click on **Hide Unselected**, you will isolate that selection. But if you click on **Hide Invert**, your selection will disappear and what was unselected will be what is now visible.
- **Unhide**: Use this option to finish the isolation process. If you click on it, everything will be visible again.

Summary

We've just learned the basics about handling modo, moving through viewports, and working with selections. Also, we took a quick look at tab-based work and an overall walkthrough across the different tools for modeling.

You can now move on to the next chapter, where we will start to create things with the modeling tools.

2

Beginning with Modeling

Now that we know how to handle the interface, we're going to take a look at the basic principles of modeling. We will learn how to create geometry, modify it, and build our own model from scratch.

In this chapter, we will cover the following topics:

- What's under the modeling tab?
- Basic Modeling
- Modifying your mesh
- Making copies
- Editing the mesh
- Working with vertices
- Working with edges

What's under the modeling tab?

This first part will cover the main procedures to work with when you are in the modeling phase.

modo is a well known tool for modeling that stands out from the rest of the 3D packages. As a modeler, you will find many simple and clever tools for (at first) hard-to-complete tasks. In this chapter you will see some tips to keep your work organized along with basic manipulations of your scene and a bunch of tools you can use to help your modeling workflow.

Layers – organizing your scene

Before you start looking at the different tools and methods of modeling, it's a good idea to have a look at the item's panel, which is located in the top-right part of the screen. This panel is a must if you want to keep your scene organized. modo uses a layers system for that, the same as Photoshop.

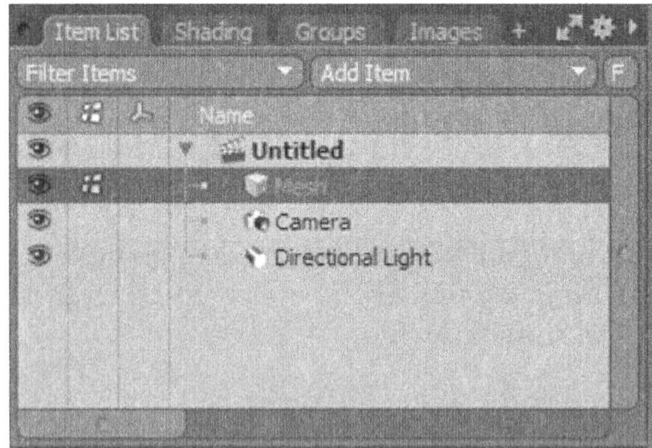

So you will be able to group certain parts of your model into a separate layer. Remember, always be well organized and methodical if you don't want to lose control of you model.

By default, this panel shows three different items, labeled with a well recognizable icon, as shown in the preceding screenshot. It's a nested system, so you can group items into folders and subfolders. This works exactly as a regular file browser: click an element to select it, *Ctrl* + click for multiple selections, and *Shift* + click for a ranged selection. You can group a selection by pressing the *G* key.

You can also move elements up and down the items tree if you want your elements visually grouped, or if you want to move them in or out of a folder.

Let's take a closer look at what is in this panel:

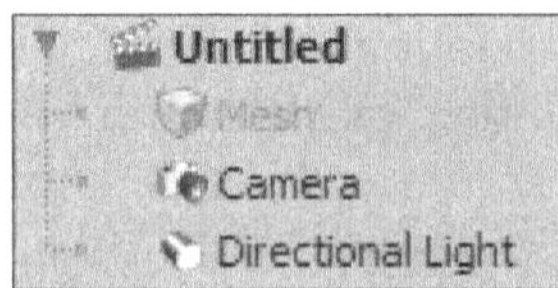

- **Mesh**: A mesh is basically a layer that contains your model, or parts of it.
- **Camera**: We will discuss the camera in its own section, but basically, this is the camera you will use to take a shot of your scene, as you would in real life.
- **Directional Light**: There is only one light in a fresh new scene, and it's of the directional type unless you change it. We will not touch it now, just keep in mind that it is there for further use.

Moving, scaling, and rotating

This is an essential part of the modeling process. Apart from selecting things, the moving/scaling/rotating action is something that you will be doing most of the time:

These tools—technically named **linear operators**—act over the selection you have made and are controlled by an axis-based overlay showing different shapes depending on what action you're calling. You have the following four choices:

- **Move** (shortcut: *W*): This tool lets you move your selection in the 3D space across the three different axis. You can choose to move it snapped to a particular axis if you use the handles, or move it freely if you just drag-and-drop while the tool is active. Once the move action is complete, just hit the Space bar to deselect it:

The move tool

- **Rotate** (shortcut: *E*): This works the same as the move tool, but it rotates the selection across any axis you choose:

The rotate tool

- **Scale** (shortcut: *R*): The same again, but now the action will be scaling the model. You can act over one particular axis. Let's say you drag the x axis in the scale tool; you will see how your model stretches or squeezes (depending on if you drag in one or other direction), while the rest of the axis remain untouched. You can also scale the mesh uniformly if you use the central circle of the tool, which will act over the three axes at the same time:

The scale tool

- **Transform** (shortcut: *Y*): This is the three tools combined in to a single one. If you choose it, you will be able to move, rotate, or scale the model without needing to switch between the tools:

The transform tool

Action centers

An **action center** is the point from where the action will take place. By default, the action center will be the same as the volumetric center of the selection, but you can customize it in many ways.

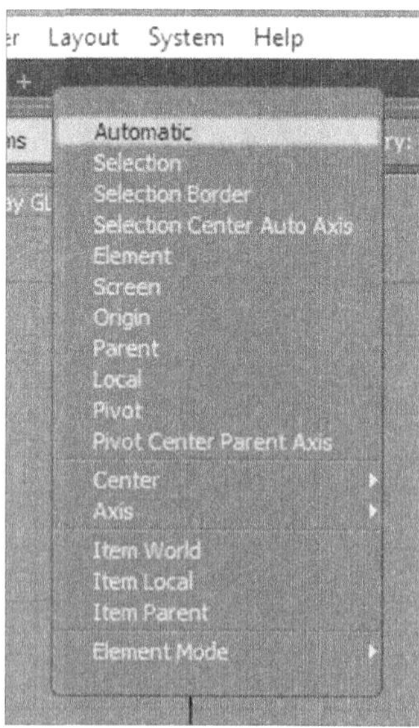

There are several options for this, but for now, we will focus on only three of them, which I find more practical:

- Automatic: It's the default action center. The action will take place from the volumetric center of the model.
- Selection: The action center will be recalculated depending on what you have selected, so the axis of the tool you choose will not be the same as the x, y, and z of the 3D space; they will align with what you have selected. This is useful for moving something along its own facing direction.
- Custom action center: This option is not present in the action center menu, because it's always available to the user. Once you select a tool, you can work on its own handles where they are (volumetric center of the selection), but you can also set a different position for it. Maybe you want to scale an object while it's still standing on the floor: You select the Scale tool and click on the area where the chair meets the floor, so the handles will be placed there. If you click-and-drag the center circle of the tool, you will see how the chair scales up and down from the point you have established, thus not loosing contact with the floor.

Falloffs

Falloffs are a very interesting way of modifying things. In short, it works combined with the tool you select; indicating it to affect certain parts more than others.

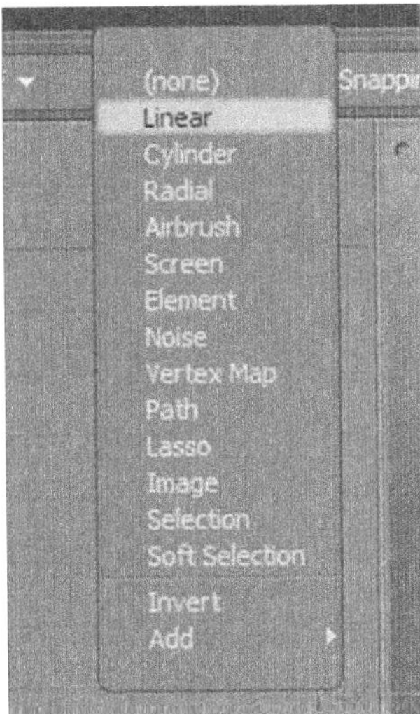

That way you can set a linear falloff, a circular one, or whatever that suits your needs in that moment. The way to use falloffs is by clicking on its button and selecting the type of the falloff you want. There are many, but for now we will just look at the two you will be using more:

- **Linear**: A linear falloff makes a tool's effect more "intensive" along a distance defined by the falloff, in a completely linear way.
- **Radial**: The intensity of the tool affected by the falloff is ruled by a circular shape, where the most you get away from its center, the more influence will have the tool.

Work planes

Take a look at your perspective viewport. You will see two grids filling it. One is dark and horizontal—some kind of a virtual floor. The other is of a light color and intersects the first one. This white grid is what we call the work plane.

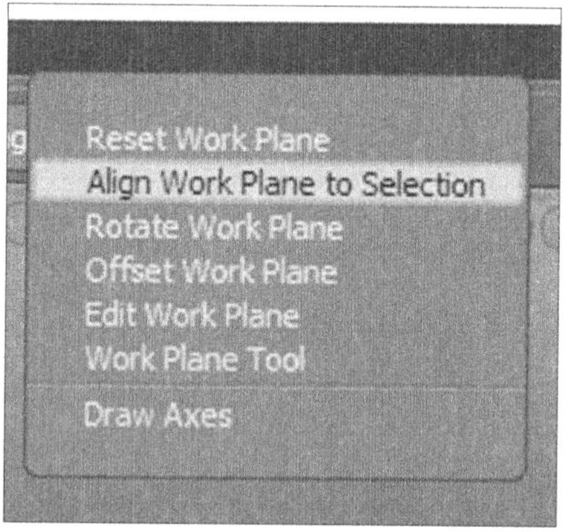

The work plane is the plane you are working on, that is your canvas. If you rotate your view, you will see how there comes a moment where the work plane changes to fit the view you are using. If you rotate the view to face the floor, the work plane will change to remain the best it can facing your view.

Now rotate the view until the work plane becomes vertical. Click on the **Cube Primitive** button (**Basic** tab of the toolbox) then click-and-drag in the work plane. You are now drawing a square that is somehow "attached" to the work plane, which is acting like a canvas for your drawing. The same way if you want to draw it on the floor, rotate the view until the work plane becomes a horizontal floor. The limitation of the work plane is that it only changes to fit one of the three axis (x, y, or z).

There will be situations where the standard work plane will not be usable. Imagine you have a cube that is rotated, that is, its faces are not facing correctly on any of the three axes. If you want to draw a square on one of its faces, you will have two ways of doing this: you can either draw a square and then rotate it to manually match the cube rotation, or you can use the work plane. The procedure will be as follows:

Select the face of the cube where you want to draw the square, then click on the **Work Plane** button, and from the menu, select **Align Work Plane to Selection**. You will see how the work plane changes to fit exactly the orientation of the face selected. From now on, you can draw the square in that face, knowing that it will be perfectly aligned with the cube. Once you've finished drawing, just click again in the work plane menu and select **Reset Work Plane**.

Basic modeling

This will be the core part of the modeling phase. We will see the needed tools to create and modify your own scene. The following is the most important things you will find under the **Basic** tab:

Primitives

The first thing we must learn to start modeling is what we call primitives. In short words, there are two methods for creating geometry: You can create it from zero or else you can start your model by basing it on a primitive, or group of primitives.

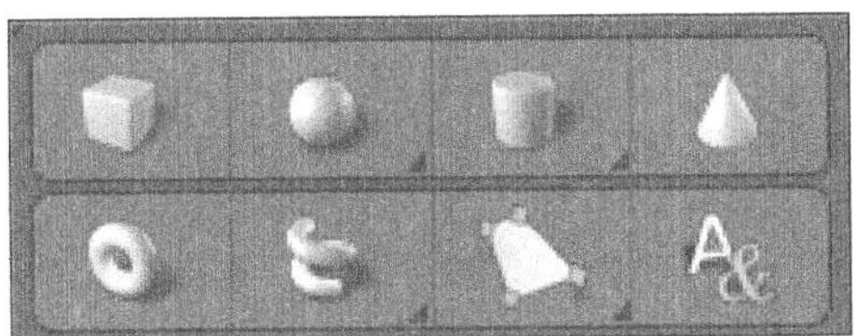

But, what is a primitive? Think about the most basic 3D bodies. We have cubes, cylinders, spheres, and things like that, right? Those are primitives, basic bodies that you can generate quickly. In modo there are several primitives, but for a basic modeling, we will only need the most basic ones:

- **Cube**: You know this already; it is a 6-faced body shaped like a dice.
- **Sphere**: A sphere, or a ball if you prefer.
- **Teapot**: Sorry... what? Yes, a teapot, literally. We will not be using teapot shapes for modeling, but, even if you find it weird, we will use it later in the material and rendering phase, so for now, just keep in mind there is a teapot.

The procedure to generate the primitives is basically always the same, and there are two ways:

- Drawing a primitive: Regardless of what primitive you want to create, the steps are, in general terms, drawing the base and the adding the extra dimension that makes it volumetric. For example, if you want to draw a cube, you must click on the **Cube** button, and then click-and-drag in your work plane to draw the base and then pull the handle corresponding to its height. Once you have the required shape, click on space to drop the tool. Of course you can always interrupt the creation process by hitting the Space bar. Let's say if you want to generate a simple plane, you can use the cube tool too, drawing the base and then dropping the tool:

Standard primitive creation buttons

- Generating a unit primitive: Instead of clicking on the **Primitive** button, if you use *Ctrl* + click, you will generate a unit primitive. This means that, without the need to draw it, a standard sized primitive will be automatically generated in the very center of the 3D space:

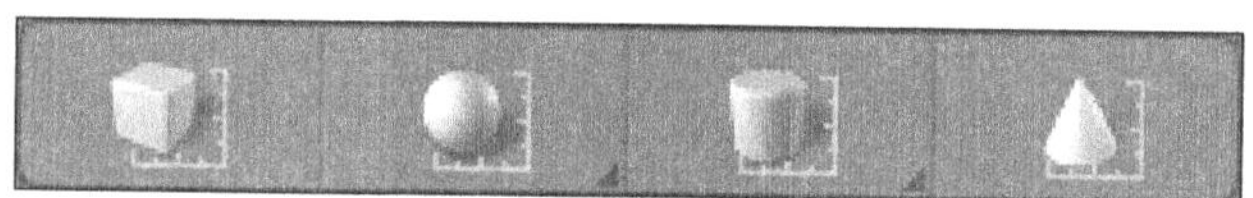

Unit primitive creation buttons (with Ctrl key pressed)

Free form shapes

Instead of working with primitives, we can work with free form shapes, that is, shapes defined by you, not restricted to simple spheres or cubes:

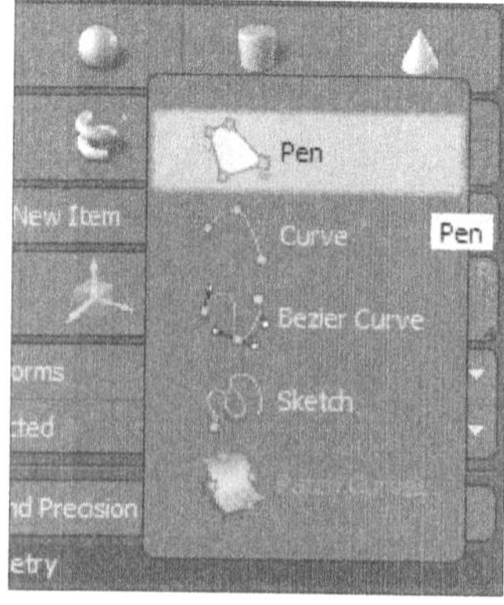

This will give us more control and freedom when creating our model. We are still in the **Basic** tab, but this time we will focus on the Pen tool.

The **Pen** tool might seem basic at first, but you will find this will become a very useful tool for your modeling. Let's have a look at it.

When you click in the **Pen** tool, you will see that as with every other tool, a bunch of options in the bottom of the panel. The main option we will see for the Pen tool is the one labeled as **Make Quads**.

In the preceding screenshot, you will see how the **Make Quads** option affects the behavior of the tool. The first polygon was generated without the **Make Quads** option enabled, so you just have to go placing points one after another, and a polygon will be created as you place them. When you have your polygon the way you want, hit the Space bar to drop the tool and you're done.

The second one is different. It was created with the **Make Quads** option enabled. If you go placing points one by one, you will see that a squared polygon will be automatically generated. The first three points must be placed in order; so you place (for example) the top-left point, then the bottom-right point, and finally the bottom-left point; and in that moment, a quad (as we call the four-sided polygons) will be generated. From that moment you can simply go placing points one after another, and a new quad will be generated on each click, resulting in a shape similar to what you see in the screenshot. This option is handy for creating stripes of polygons.

The Subdivide tool

The Subdivide tool is very useful for refining your mesh, giving it more definition. The way to use it is by selecting the mesh you want to smooth and clicking on the **SDS Subdivide** button:

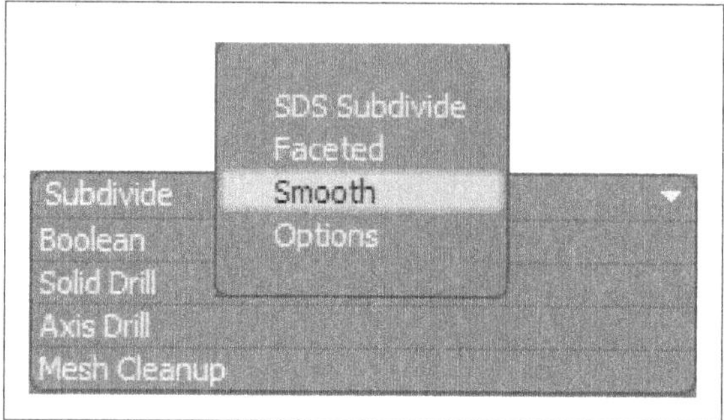

You see two spheres in the following screenshot: the one on the left is unsmoothed (as it's a unit primitive) and the one on the right is after the subdivision has been applied. Looks way more smooth, but it's also heavier (it's got much more polygons).

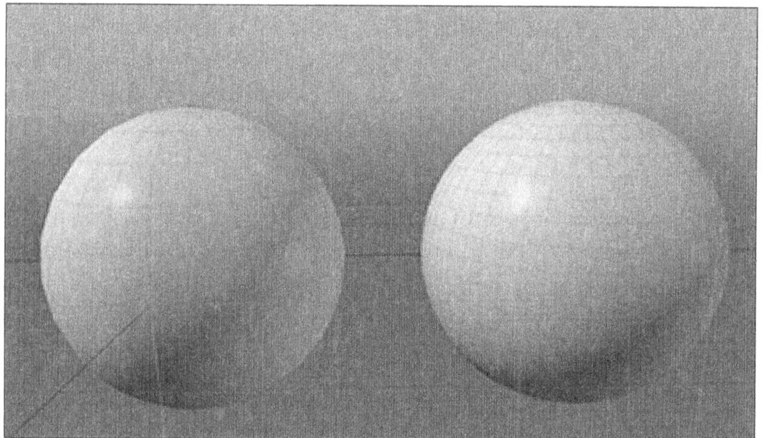

Basically, what this tool does is multiply the number of polygons of your mesh by four. It takes each polygon and splits it vertically and horizontally, and applies a smoothing on each subdivision, so you will get a denser and smoother mesh. You can use this tool to make boxy meshes look like they are smooth. You can apply the tool the number of times you want to give your mesh more and more definition, but be careful, because the more polygons you have, the heavier the mesh will be, and your scene will be harder to handle. As a general rule, use the amount of definitions you need, and no more.

The Bevel tool

Applied to faces, edges, or vertices, this tool will let you smooth edges with a custom definition; inset or offset faces and round corners when applied to vertices:

The Bevel tool

This is a tool I use a lot. You can use the tool in Polygon mode as well as in Edge mode. By now, we will see its effects in the Polygon mode (the Edge Bevel tool will need a more extensive explanation later):

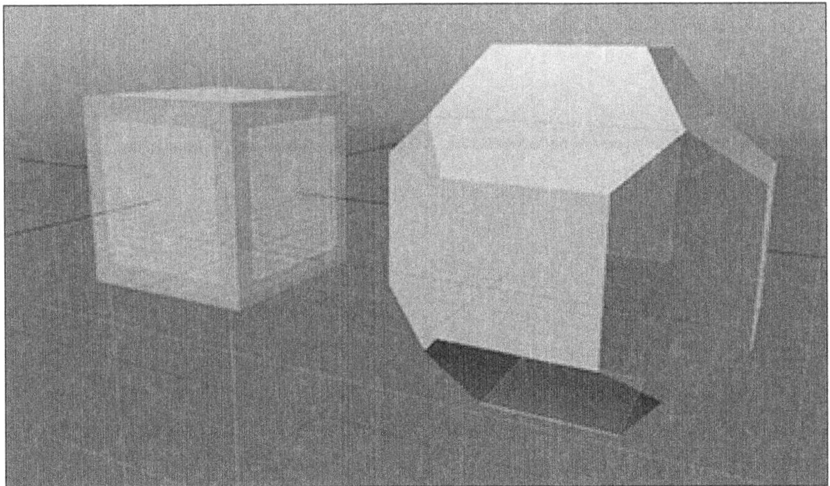

To use this tool, you must select a polygon, or group of them and click on the button. Once it's clicked, you will see the following two handles to control the effect:

- **Inset**: This is the red handle. It controls how much the polygon is contracted or expanded.
- **Shift**: This is the blue handle. It controls how much the polygon is shifted in or out of its original position.

In the preceding screenshot, you can see a cube after the Bevel tool has been applied. In the first cube, I only beveled in its faces, so you see the effect, creating in fact new geometry around them. The second cube is exactly the same, but in this case I applied a shift value too, so the faces are beveled in and then shifted out. You can choose to just bevel or bevel and shift.

The Extrude tool

With this tool you can generate new geometry by extending faces:

This one is a classic. An **extrusion** is a shift applied to a polygon, so you make that polygon shift out of its original mesh. Imagine a skyscraper rising up from the ground, or a floor plan expanding up so the walls start appearing. You get the idea?

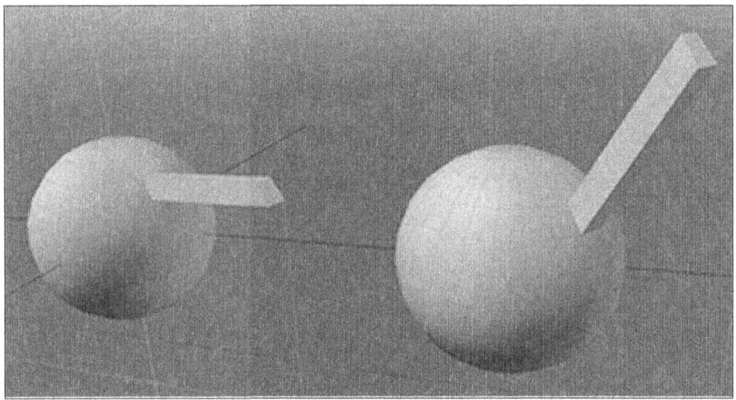

To use this tool, select a polygon, click on the tool, and extrude the polygon along one of the axes (using the relevant handle). You can also extrude it freely, without being constrained to an axis, by dragging outside the handles. In this case, the work plane will rule the direction of the extrusion.

There are many uses for this tool, but, as in the example I gave you, you will use it very often when you have your floor plan modeled, and you extrude it up to make the walls.

The Bridge tool

This tool connects the edges of faces with the new geometry:

When dealing with a bit complex shapes, the Bridge tool will prove to be very handy. What it does is connect two polygons (or a group of polygons), in fact making a real bridge; that is, creating geometry in the process.

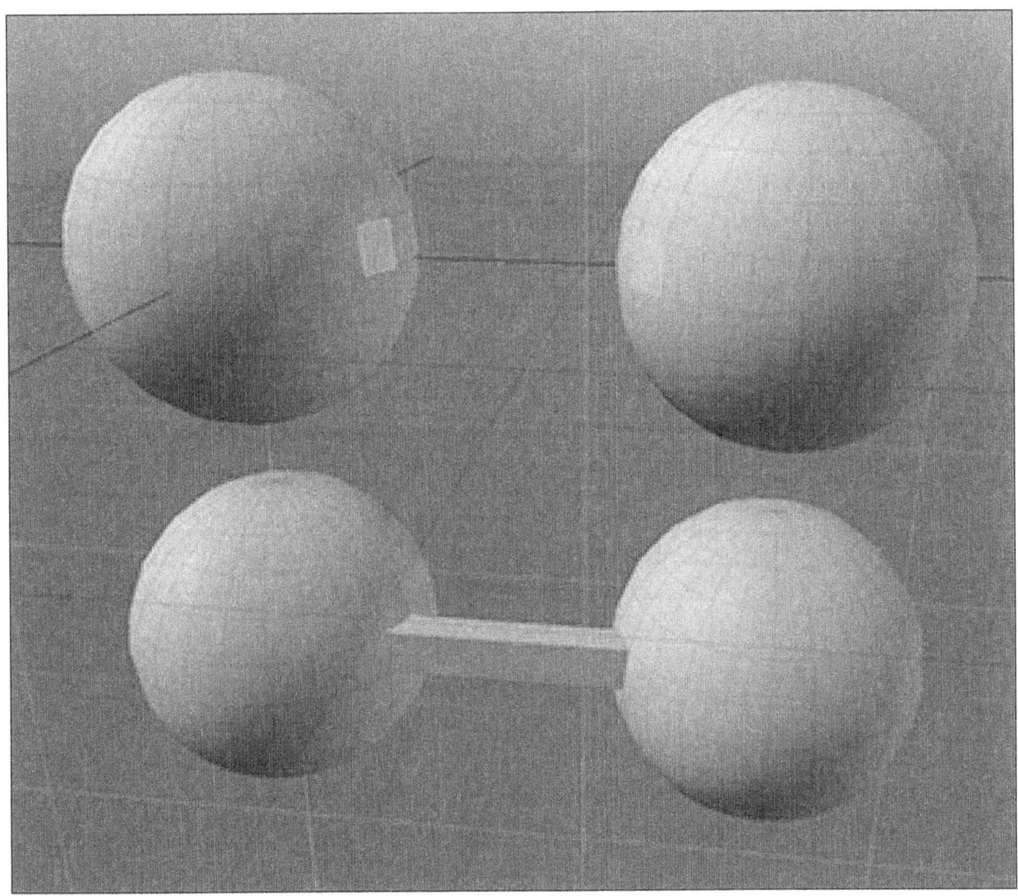

To use it, select the two polygons and click on the tool. They will get connected by a bridge of polygons that can be tweaked in the tool options, where you can define the number of segments of the bridge, some curvature if it's needed, and so on.

In the previous screenshot, you can see the process explained clearly: first we select two polygons, then we click on the tool, and the bridge appears connecting them.

The Slice tool

With the **Slice** tool, you can make cuts to your mesh, thus modifying the geometry and creating new polygons from the existing ones:

This tool acts like a knife. It lets you literally cut a mesh just by defining the cut. When you click on the tool, working preferably in an orthographic view for more controllable results, just define the cut placing the start and end of it, and drop the tool. The result will be your mesh sliced exactly as you defined.

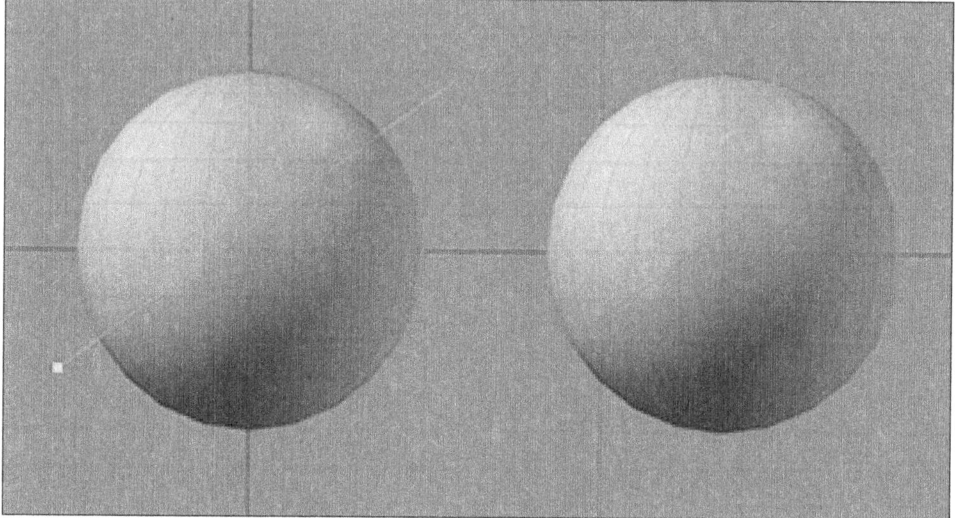

The Thicken tool

The **Thicken** tool lets you add some thickness to a polygon or group of polygons:

This one is a very cool tool, one of my most used. It lets you give thickness to a flat polygon or a group of them. Just select the polygons, click on the tool and drag the blue handle to thicken it:

You may be wondering how this is different to using the **Extrude** tool. Well, the Extrude tool, as you read before, is good for thickening a mesh in certain cases. In general, flat surfaces, with all their polygons facing more or less (or exactly) to the same direction are more suitable to work with the **Extrude** tool, but the Thicken tool "reads" the differences of every polygon (in terms on where they are facing to) and make some kind of adaptive extrusion, meaning that there will be no overlapping, confusing geometry, and so on.

Think that you have modeled a t-shirt. It's done and it has no thickening at all. Will you use the Extrude tool? Absolutely not. A t-shirt is a very complex shape, with lots of polygons facing to different, and sometimes opposite, directions. Also, the **Extrude** tool will only thicken the mesh in one single direction. Instead of that, use the **Thicken** tool. Just click the tool and drag. Your mesh will get some thickening perfectly adapted to each corner or surface of the mesh. That's the power of this tool.

Modifying your mesh

In this section we will explain some tools you will use to make some tweaking to your mesh, apart from moving, scaling, or rotating it.

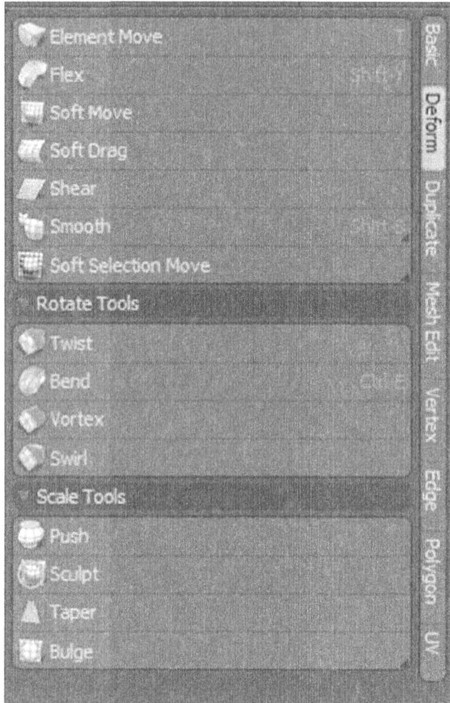

We will focus more on advanced tools that will make complex deformations simple, such as bending things or free-hand manipulating a mesh.

The Element move tool

This tool lets you freehand move or drag geometry for general modifications of the mesh:

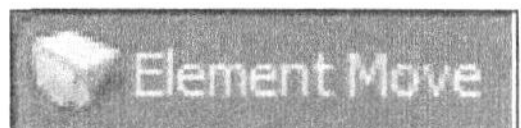

You're going to love this one. We are moving apart from the axis-based tools and getting a bit into a more "organic" workflow. The Element Move tool is for moving things, but in a different and more interesting way:

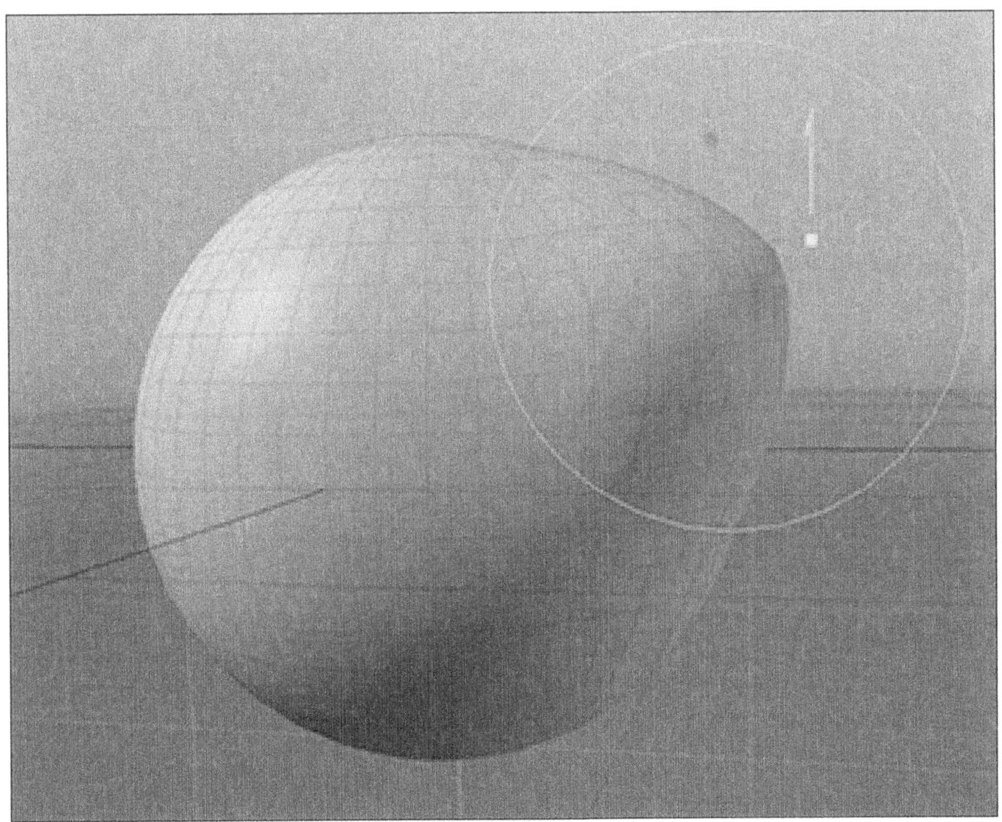

It works something like a soft pinch. When selected, you can right-click and drag to adjust its area of influence. Then you just drag parts of your model that will deform with a radial falloff applied, so you get that soft and natural deformation. This is very useful if you want to make some general tweaks to your model, especially if it's something organic.

As an example, you can have the model of a human face, and you're asked to tweak the face so it shows an angry expression. That is a perfect case to use the Element Move tool. Set a big size and start dragging here and there to get the shape you want. You will see how the geometry of the face changes in a very natural and soft looking way. It surely makes your life easier.

See the following screenshot: from a default face model, I used the Element Move tool to get a kind of angry expression; done in like 10 seconds:

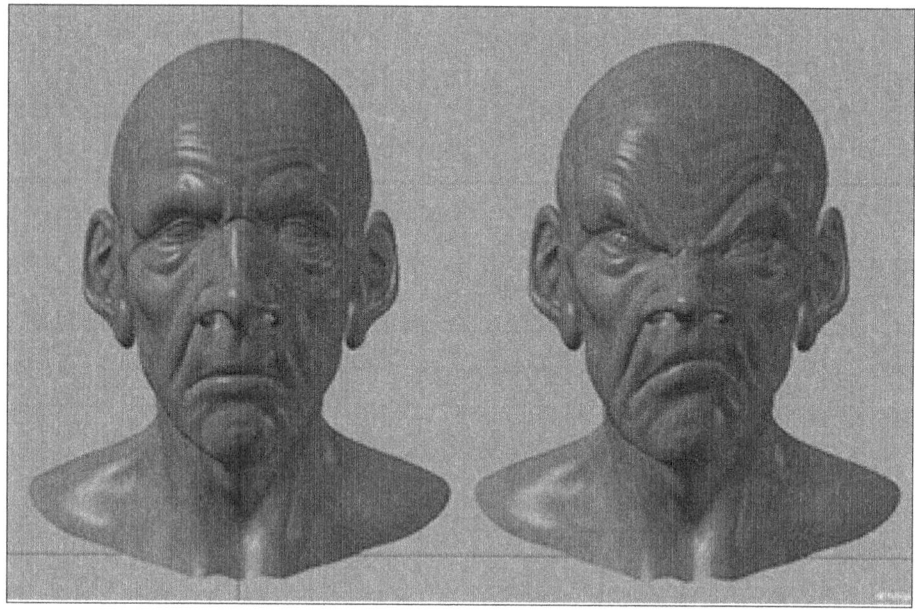

The Flex tool

With the **Flex** tool, you will be able to bend your mesh from an articulated point, as if it were a joint:

When dealing with articulated models, we have resources in the model phase to pose things a little. The **Flex** tool comes to fill this need. What it does is flex a shape based on a selection.

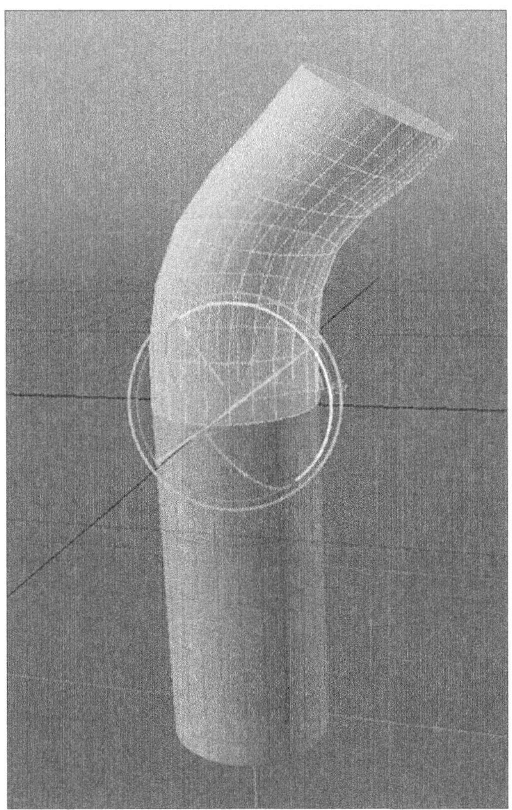

Take a look at the preceding screenshot. I generated a cylinder, but think of it as an arm. You have a human arm modeled and you want to flex it by the elbow. To do that, select the part of the arm you want to flex, and leave the rest unselected. When you activate the tool, you will see a handle to control the deformation. Make use of the rotational handles to flex the shape the way you want. You can control the definition of the flexing with the **Steps** box located in the tool's **Properties** panel (located in the bottom-left of the screen).

The Sculpt tool

The **Sculpt** tool will let you create elevations or depressions in the mesh, freehand and in a natural way:

One of my favorites. This one works similar as the Element Move tool, but it's more like a sculpting brush, so you can go adding or subtracting volume from your mesh. As with the Element Move tool, you must right-click and drag to set brush size then you click-and-drag over your mesh. The result is not moving things, but in fact, sculpting the mesh. The volume will grow up as you brush your model. This is great to give your model the extra punch of realism if you want to make things such as clothes, wrinkles, and so on.

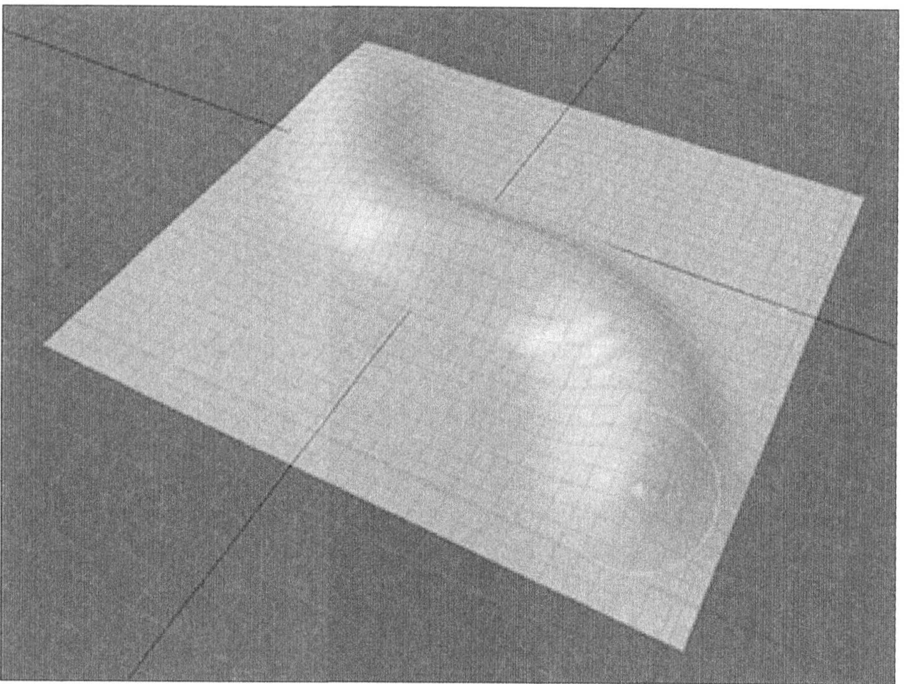

If you want to subtract instead of add volume, just use the *Ctrl* key to invert the effect. Combined with the Element Move tool, it's an awesome pair of tools to make general adjustments to your model.

Making copies

In this section we will see some tools for duplicating things. There are certain cases when you will need to work in scenes that will contain many copies of the same object, due to the own nature of the scene. Things such as a cinema hall (with a lot of seats), or a classroom (with a desk for every student), or in general, scenarios where you will have to deal with numerous copies of identical elements will get benefit from using the tools shown in the following screenshot:

The Mirror tool

Mirroring is the operation of duplicating an object, making it symmetrical to the original one. This is the tool for it:

This tool is very appropriate when working with symmetrical models, such as faces. But there are more situations where you will find symmetry without such advanced modeling as a human face. Think about a bed with two night tables on each side, a set of headphones, a lot of furniture designs... symmetry is all around us:

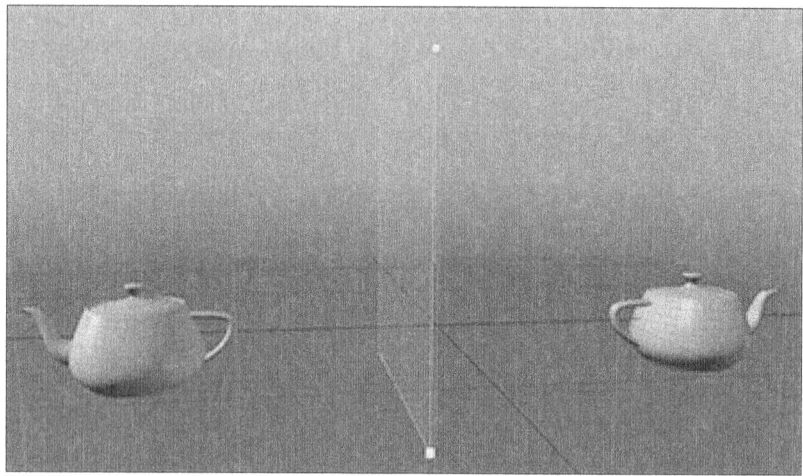

The easiest way to apply symmetry is doing it based on an axis. If you have your model perfectly centered, the axis of it will be the same as the axis of the 3D space, which is the default for this tool. So, select what you want to mirror, tick the axis you want your mirroring into and click on **Apply**. The action will complete in the same way that you can see in the preceding screenshot.

The Clone tool

Under the **Duplicate** tab, you can find this very useful tool for making copies quickly and easily.

This is another way to duplicate things without the need to copy/paste each element:

If you click on this tool, you will see a handle with three axes like in the rest of the tools, and if you drag any of them, a clone of the original mesh will be generated (based on the number of copies you state in the tool's properties). There are two methods of generating a clone line:

- **Additive method**: It's the default for this tool. Drag the handle to establish the distance you want between each copy, and then go increasing the number of copies in the tool's properties, so you will get a line of clones that becomes longer as you raise the number.
- **Ranged method**: If you tick the **between** checkbox in the tool's properties, the generation method will change, because now the copies of the original mesh will be generated between the original and the last copy. So, the way to work with this method will be establishing the final length of the clone line, and then start increasing the number of copies in the tool's **Properties** panel. The clones will be generated all through the length you defined, using uniform gaps.

Making arrays

This one is a powerful tool for duplicating objects, more complex than cloning or copy/pasting geometry:

An array is a matrix. It's a more advanced version of the Clone tool, since the Clone tool lets you make copies in a linear pattern, the array tool is good to expand the copies along the three axes, in a 3-dimensional pattern. It works more or less like the Clone tool, but if you go dragging the handles, you will control every dimension of the cloning independently:

The amount of copies for each axis can be controlled too by the **Properties** panel of the tool. There are the following two variations of this:

- **Array**: It makes copies linearly across all the three axes.
- **Radial array**: It works in a radial pattern, instead of a linear one. Choose the axis you want your array to align to and set the number of copies and degrees to be covered. The numbers around a clock are a perfect example of radial cloning.

Editing the mesh

The **Mesh Edit** tab contains several tools for, in general terms, adding geometry to your mesh to go on adding more detail.

Let me show you the most interesting and useful tools you will find here:

Curve Slice and Loop Slice

Slicing a mesh can be a good method of defining more interesting shapes. Let's take a look at how to use this tool.

The following screenshot shows the use of the **Curve Slice** tool. As you can see, you can make cuts with curvy shapes:

Viewing your mesh from a non-perspective view (better for this tool), start drawing a curve by placing points. That curve will be the final shape of the cut. Once you have it the way you want it, drop the tool and you will see the mesh is cut to that shape.

This second screenshot shows the use of the Loop Slice tool. This tool makes a slice call across a loop of polygons. The easiest use would be selecting an edge to cut across it. When you click on the tool, a slice will be generated across the entire loop corresponding to that edge.

It's a very customizable tool. In its **Properties** panel you will find options to set the kind of slice you want, numbers of it, and so on. The main variations for this tool are:

- **Count**: Use this parameter to establish the number of slices you need.
- **Symmetry**: One the slicing modes. It places the cuts symmetrically along the loop sliced.
- **Free**: While generating the slice, you can freely move it in order to place it where you need it.
- **Uniform**: This places the slices uniformly, so the loop gets sliced into equal parts.

Booleans

This is a classic operation in 3D modeling. Although it can generate some thrash geometry, it is always good to know how to use it and when:

Boolean

A Boolean is an operation where you combine two meshes, getting a result depending on if the combination is an addition, a subtraction, and so on. In simple words, it is like adding one mesh to another, or subtracting one from another. Booleans are a quick way to get more complex shapes. If you look at the following screenshot, you will see a typical Boolean subtract operation, where I have subtracted part of a sphere from a cube:

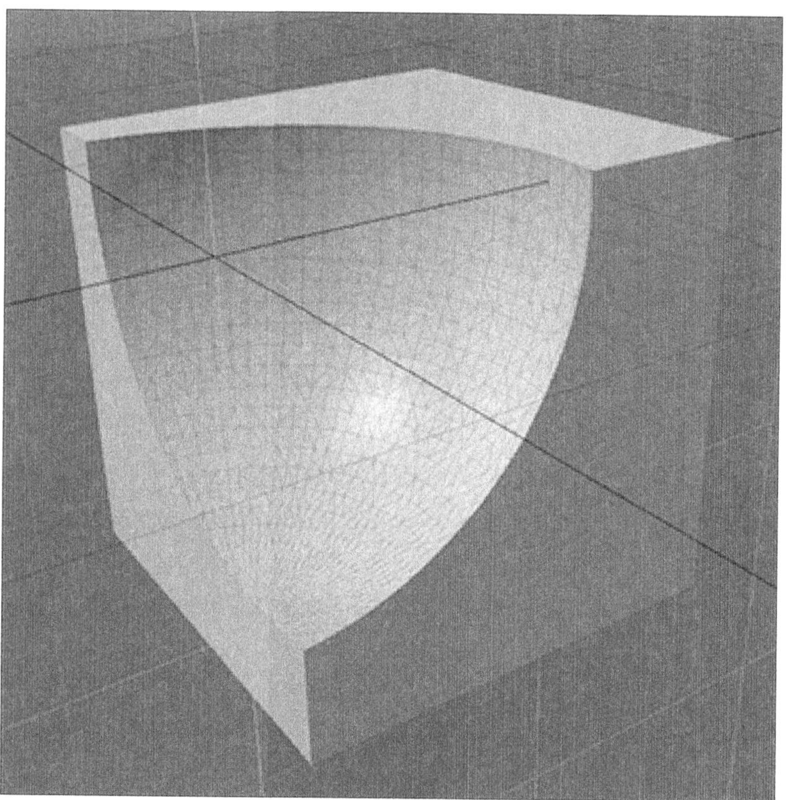

Let's take a look at the different kind of Booleans we have available in modo:

- **Add**: You add one mesh to another, resulting in a combined mesh.
- **Subtract**: You subtract the volume of one mesh from the other, usually resulting in holes and cavities.
- **Intersect**: The resulting mesh will be the common volume between the two involved meshes. As the new states, where they intersect.

The way to use this tool is as follows:

1. First you must have two meshes. We will call them A (passive mesh) and B (active mesh). This means that B will act over A, and they will each be in its separate layer.
2. Then activate the **Boolean** tool. From the pop-up dialog, you can choose the Boolean type you need, accept it, and the operation will be done, giving you the result depending on the type you selected.

In general terms, Booleans are not the best way if you want to get a clean flowing mesh, because it's an automatic process and there will be situations where it doesn't work quite well due to the generation of trash geometry, or problems with the geometry itself. This would happen in complex meshes, but the tool will work very nicely when simpler meshes are involved.

In the following screenshot, you will see the result of each different Boolean between a sphere and a cube (from left-to-right: original meshes, add, subtract, and intersect):

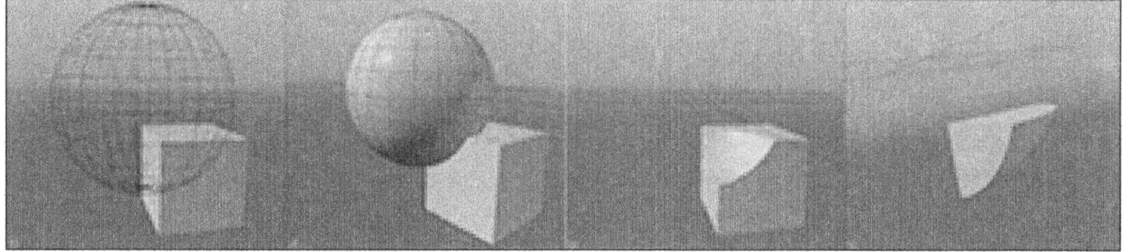

Drills

You can make holes or project cuts on your mesh with this tool:

Although there are various drill tools, we will focus on the **Axis Drill** tool.
If the Boolean tool is useful to make holes in solid meshes, the drill tool does the same, but it's more efficient when trying to modify flat planes (or not enclosed meshes in general):

The same principle is applied: have your two meshes in separate layers and pick the drill mode you need. The passive mesh will be drilled with the shape of the active mesh. The following are the different drilling methods you can use:

- **Tunnel**: Makes an empty hole in the mesh.
- **Core**: The opposite to the tunnel mode. Removes everything out of the drilling shape in the passive mesh.
- **Stencil**: Makes a cut, not removing anything.

Examine how the different methods work (from left-to-right: tunnel, core and stencil):

Mesh Cleanup

A nice help when refining your mesh is the **Mesh Cleanup** tool. It will do all the tedious work for you:

Mesh Cleanup

This is a great tool in many ways. It literally cleans a mesh, looking for errors, overlapping polygons, wrong faces, and lots of other things and fixes everything.

Keep in mind that although it's a great tool, it's not a magic wand. It's an automatic process, and means that it can work, but not perfectly. I personally use it to clean an imported mesh from other software. Given that exporting to another format usually generates a lot of trash geometry or errors, especially when working with complex models, this tool is a must-have right after loading that exported file.

You can too use it to make an automatic check of your mesh, if you feel (or see) that there is something wrong that you cannot point at.

Working with vertices

In this section, we will see how we can work the vertices individually using the tools available under the **Vertex** tab:

Centering

In order to have a well organized mesh, it's important to work with the centering tool that will align your selection. Using the centering tool applied to vertices is always a good idea, because vertices gives you more control at the time of selecting areas from your model. Selecting an area using polygons or edges can give you certain troubles because they are not really too precise, but vertices are. So, my advice is to use the Vertex mode with this tool:

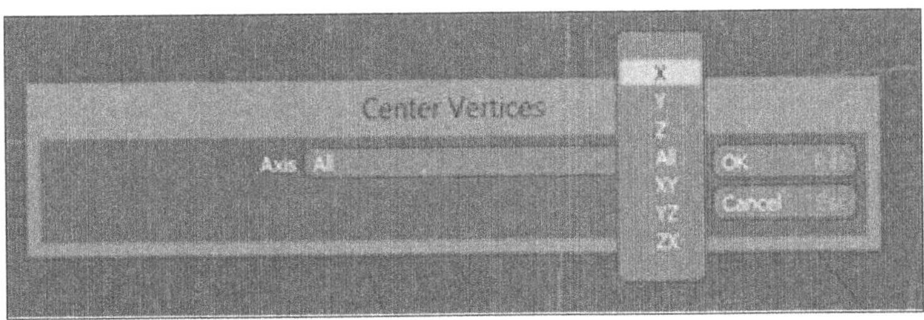

To use it, make a selection of the vertices you want to center and click on the tool. The pop-up dialog will ask you for the axis (or group of axis) you want them aligned to. Select the one you need and click on **OK**. Then your selection will be aligned to the very center of the axis selected.

You also have an extra tool for this, located just under the **Center Vertices** tool called **Center All Axis**. It's some kind of shortcut to a complete centering. If you click on this tool, your selection will be aligned to the very center of the 3D space.

Setting position

In case you need to align your selection of vertices completely, you have the **Set Vertex Position** tool that sets the same exact value to every pixel across the axis you choose. This particular tool is always very useful to align offsetted vertices. You can be modeling something that needs to be totally flat by just eyeballing the placement of the vertices. Then select the surface that you want to be flat and apply this tool to make sure all the vertices involved are exactly at the same value:

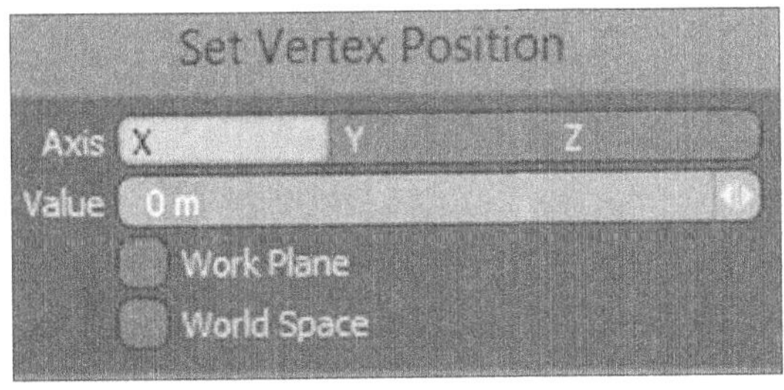

Merging

This tool is related to cleaning a mesh. After a work session, it is not unusual for you (as a human) make mistakes. There can be some overlapping vertices, some trash geometry, maybe you forgot to weld some parts, and so on. This tool will help you to merge every group of vertices that are overlapping. You can use it too, for welding parts of the model in an automated manner.

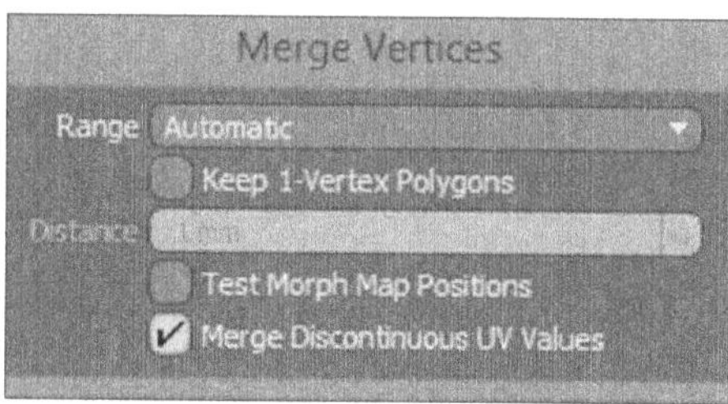

You have the following two options for this tool:

- **Automatic**: It merges vertices automatically and is based in a default threshold distance. It normally works well.
- **Fixed**: It does the same thing, but is based on a user-defined threshold, in case you want this tool to be more exhaustive, merging vertices that are a little more offsetted than the default distance.

Working with edges

To finish the modeling section, we will see the tools related to edges. We will be mainly using three of the tools, which are the basics for starting your work. Personally, I find working the edges is a great method of modeling, and these tools will help release the potential of them.

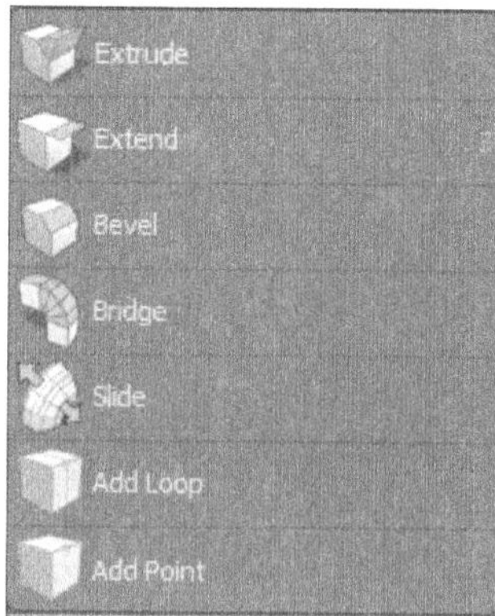

Bevel

Don't waste time manually smoothing and refining edges. This tool will do it for you quick and easy:

The edge beveling is something very useful in order to get nice details or solve more or less complex situations. When you apply this tool, the edges selected from the model will get a nice bevel that you can control using the handle. The more you drag, the bigger the bevel. Also, in the **Properties** panel you can control certain aspects of the action, being the main parameter the "round level", which in fact is the number of subdivisions of the beveling. The more the number of levels, the more defined the beveling will be.

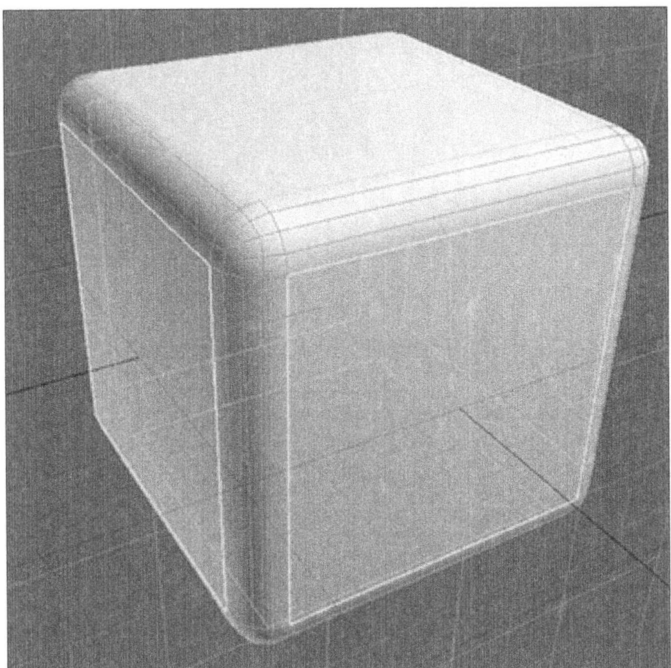

Bridge

With this tool, you can connect an edge or a group of it with another, creating new faces in the process:

Bridging edges is also a great option when modeling. It lets you connect parts of the model automatically. To bridge two edges, simply select them and click on the tool to get them connected. One of the quick ways to do this is, when the selection is done, right-click on one of the edges and select **Bridge** from the context menu:

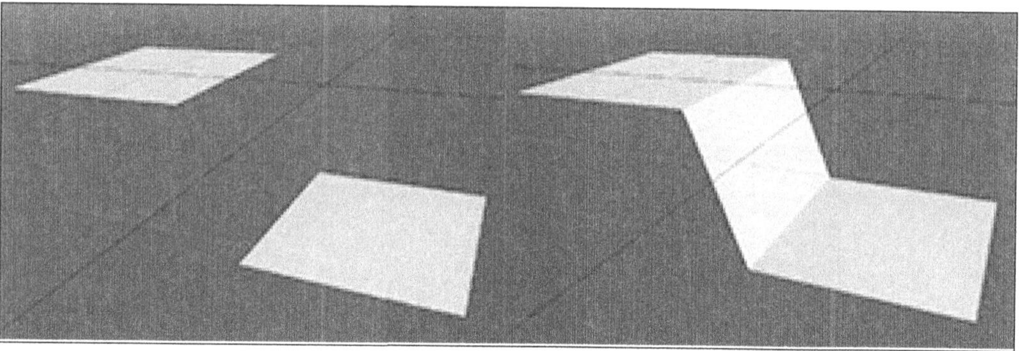

Slide

If you are refining your mesh, this tool is great to make your work easier:

This one is a tool to modify the placement of an edge or a group of them. The main benefit of this tool is that you can move edges in a non-destructive way, so they will preserve the main topology of the mesh in the best way possible.

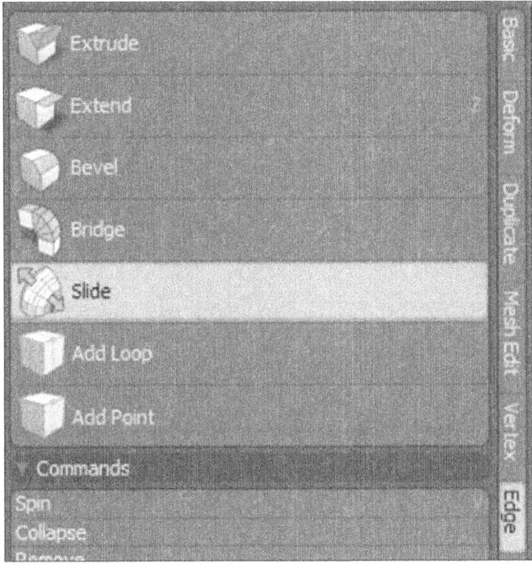

The most common case to use this tool is when you need to replace an entire loop of edges. This can be done easily and securely with this tool. Select the edge loop you want to slide (remember that double-click an edge selects all the loops), then click on the tool and drag in the visor. You will see how the loop slides back and forth without distorting the mesh (or at least not distorting it very much).

Summary

After some practicing with the tools and tips provided in this chapter, you should be now ready to create your own basic geometry. Feel free to experiment with it to transform this experience to more interesting and complex modeling projects.

For now, get yourself ready to enter the next chapter, where we will start to learn how to create materials for your scene.

3

Texturing and Materials

This is the section where we will learn how to mimic real world materials. Also, we will be using images to recreate more complex materials and learn a little about special properties of them that will make your model look the best it can.

In this chapter, we will cover the following areas:

- What is a material?
- What is a texture?
- Using materials
- Types of materials
- Using the preset library
- Special effects

What is a material?

Since this chapter deals with mimicking real world materials, we might say that a material is a set of properties of a surface that defines how they react to light. We have many different kinds of materials, categorized by whether they reflect sources of light or the environment itself, or if they are transparent in some way, or if the surface shows some bumpiness or roughness, which will make them perform very differently according to the environment around them.

What is a texture?

Before starting the explanation of the more complex aspects of textures, we should simply say that a texture is an image applied to a material. Imagine a glossy wall in a room. You will probably have some lights in the room and even a big window from where the indirect light of the exterior comes in.

As our wall is glossy, it will reflect the lights and even the environment a little bit. But there's more. You can put some textures all over it. You may also want the wall to have some cool vinyls pasted on it. You can have that and still retain the material's properties. You just need to google for a good image to be used as a texture (or you can paint or even click a picture if you have the skills or don't find what you're looking for). *Note that googling images is only right if those images are copyright-free.* Then, you can paste the image on the wall's surface to get a nice glossy wall with some vinyls on it.

Keep in mind the following main points:

- **Material**: How the surface reacts to the illumination
- **Texture**: An image (regardless if it is a procedural or a bitmap) pasted on the surface, regardless of the material type but a part of the material

If you look at the following screenshot, you will get a quick idea of the two. The model on the left shows a material while the right one shows a texture, using in fact an image of a stone wall pasted on the sphere:

Using materials

Let's now dive into the process of making good looking materials. We will look at the basic types so that you can cover a large range of real life materials, in an easy and practical way.

Creating a material

In order to create a material, we must first make a selection to assign the material to. You can apply materials either to an entire object or to a part of it. Most of the time, the material will be applied to a whole object but there are occasions when (the lesser probability) you will need to make a material only for certain areas of the object.

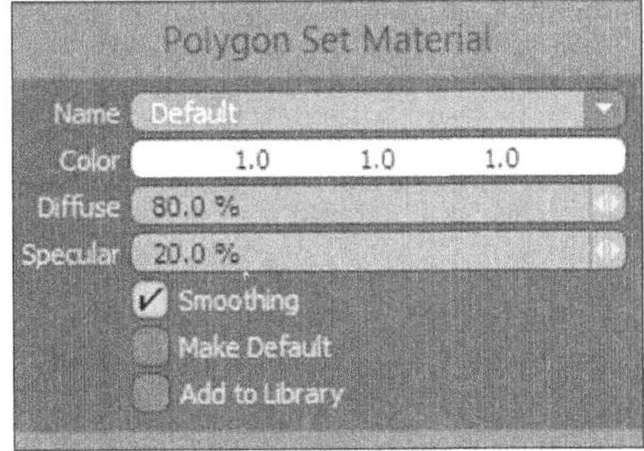

To assign a material to a selection, select faces on the object and press *M* on your keyboard. If nothing is selected, the material will be applied to the whole object. You can find the option to assign a material in the top menu under **Texture** | **Assign Material**. By default, the system will assign the name **Default** for your material, and a set of basic parameters such as **Color**, **Diffuse**, and **Specular**. Just fill in the name field with a name you like for your newly created material and click on **OK**.

Once you have your material assigned, you can check the shader tree to see how it has been included in the list of materials for your scene. In the following screenshot, you can see a new material created by me, called **new material**, shown under the **Shader Tree** option:

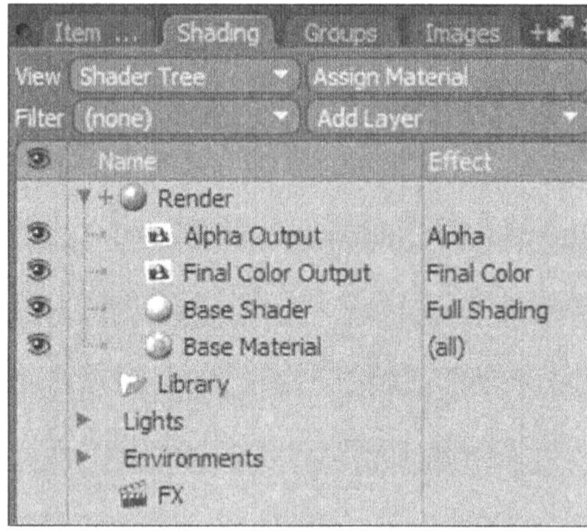

With the material created and included in the shader tree, its properties will be visible in the **Properties** panel, just under the **Shader Tree** option, when the material is selected. We will examine the properties in the next section.

Types of materials

There are four basic kinds of materials we will be discussing about. As stated before, this distinction is based on how different materials react to light.

We will learn how to decide when to use which material and how to set it up easily. The types of materials will be as follows:

- **Diffuse**: This is the most basic type of material which only shows color and no reflection or shine at all.
- **Glossy**: This type of material is useful for mimicking plastic materials or glossy surfaces, such as lacquered woods. It shows subtle reflections.
- **Specular**: In short, this is what we commonly call glass. You will always use it when creating mirrors or things made of glass in general.
- **Emitter**: This is a more advanced material that emits light. We will see just the very basics of it because this kind of material will be discussed later, in the lightning section.

Using diffuse materials

As mentioned earlier, diffuse materials are the most basic and simple kind. They show color and shading but no reflections or specularity.

Although perfect diffuse materials are rarely found in the real world, this kind of material is good to represent materials that, in general, don't show any special features such as walls, stones, bricks, and so on.

A good advice would be to set a general white diffuse material before you start creating more complex materials for your scene. Also, you can make nice renders showing only volumes and forms, such as a clay render, as you need to show only general volumes at a very early stage of production.

In the following figure, you can see how a simple white diffuse material can be used to give a general idea of the volumes at the beginning of a scene:

Using glossy materials

Glossy materials are more complex and interesting than diffuse materials. This kind of material shows reflections. There are two types of reflections depending on the nature of the material:

- **Reflection**: We call it reflection when the material reflects other objects, or the environment around it.
- **Specularity**: We call it specularity when it is the light that is reflected.

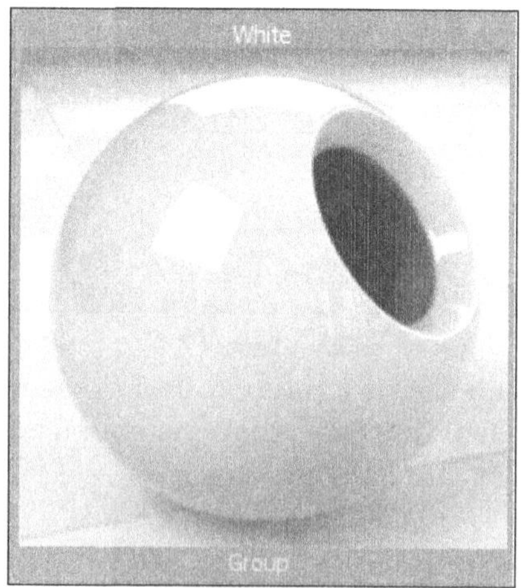

In the following figure, I have shown two materials. The sphere on the left shows specularity and the one on right shows reflection. Notice how the specular material reflects the spotlight coming from the left while the reflective material doesn't, and instead, reflects the environment:

Glossy materials are good to represent things such as porcelain, plastic, metal, mirror, and everything you can think of that shines or reflects. However, there are two exceptions: water and glass. This is exactly what the next type of materials are good for.

Using specular materials

We call specular materials to everything that act like glass. Don't get confused about the term specularity applied to glossy materials, and specular materials which are glass or water.

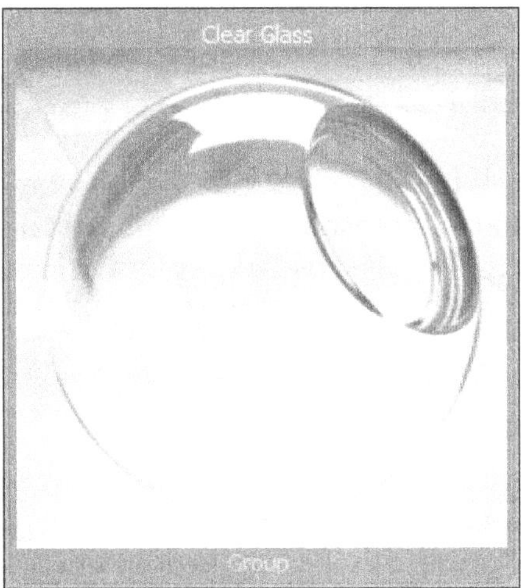

The main characteristics that define these materials are the following:

- **Transparency**: A specular material must let light travel through it. This makes it transparent in a lesser or higher degree.
- **Specularity**: As for specular materials, a specular surface reflects the light cast on it.
- **Refraction**: The light traveling through these materials always bends, distorting the objects seen through them. We call this refraction.
- **Reflection**: A specular material reflects all that surrounds it.

Notice in the previous figure how I have applied a specular material to the spherical object. Here you can see that it's transparent, reflects light and environment, as well as shows refraction, distorting what's visible through it. This fulfills the requirements to consider it as a specular material.

Using emitter materials

This type of material is very interesting when used as a light source. In other words, you can set a material that emits light, by giving it a value higher than zero in its **Luminous Intensity** field (present in the **Properties** panel of the material).

We will cover this material more deeply in *Chapter 5, Preparing a Shot*. For now, keep in mind that you will find this option needful to create all kinds of lights for your scene, apart from the specific light tools found within modo.

Understanding the base shader and base material properties

Although every material that you define in the scene has its own material properties, it is important to take a look at the **Base Shader** and **Base Material** items in your shader tree.

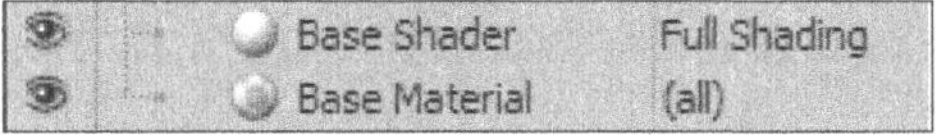

The base shader is the master controller of different aspects of general shading and visibility of the scene. Knowing that the shader tree is layer based, these elements will affect everything under them. So, you can move any other item above them to exclude them from the base shader/material.

Let's see the properties for each of them, and how can you tweak them.

The base shader properties

By clicking on the **Base Shader** item, you will see its **Properties** panel. The base shader controls general aspects of the render setup. Most of them are advanced settings related to fine-tuning the rendering, but for a beginner, I would highlight the settings explained after the following screenshot:

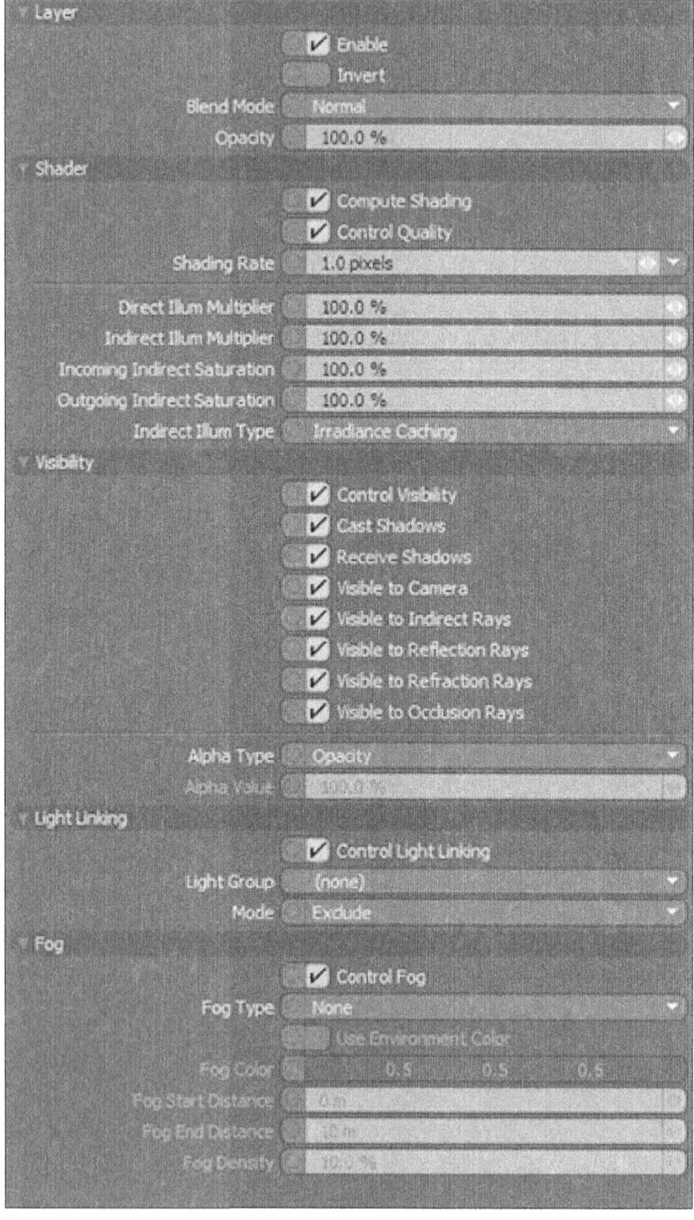

- **Enable**: Obviously, we have a checkbox to enable and disable the base shader.
- **Shading Rate**: This controls the depth of the calculated value of the shading (the number of pixels every sample is away from each other). It is always advised to decrease this value if you find it difficult to shade areas in your render, usually those that are difficult to reach by light or with a dense geometry.
- **Cast Shadows** and **Receive Shadows**: You can enable or disable shadows in your scene (only those that come from lights). This can be handy if you want to add a light that contributes to your scene, but you only want the light and not the shadows. A typical studio shot can be a good example.
- **Fog**: From the base shader, you can add and control a fog effect. I recommend you to start exploring this effect once you are comfortable with the basic tasks. It's simple to use and can give nice effects when used wisely.

The base material properties

The base material properties are the same as any other material item in the shader tree. It is a master controller of materials, and so will override any other material under it. This is useful, for example, to disable all others in the scene by dragging the base material and placing it on top of the rest of the materials. That's why it is located, by default, at the very bottom of the shader tree.

Using the preset library

Now that we know the main types of materials, it's time to learn how to create them. We have two ways for creating them that are as follows:

- **Manual creation**: When you assign a material to a surface, you can tweak its properties manually using the **Properties** panel to get the look you need.

- **Preset library**: You can also use a predefined material from the default content.

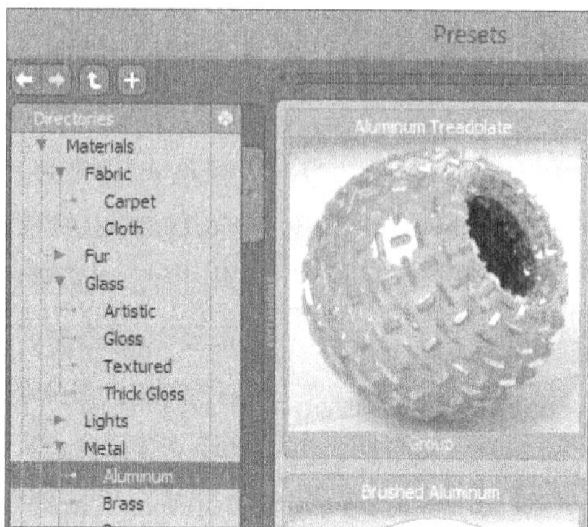

The method you choose for creating a material highly depends on its complexity. If you want a very complex material showing bumpiness, texture, and so on, you will likely want to use the preset library to cut down the time you need for creating it manually. On the other hand, if the material is to be a basic one with no special features, such as a plain porcelain material, a mirror, or a quick diffuse, you will find it more practical to use just the **Properties** panel and set up a few parameters. Your experience will tell you when to use one of the two.

To access the presets library, you must click on the **Presets** button located at the top of the **Tools** panel under the **Model** tab, **Model Quad** tab, or **Paint** tab. You can also press *F6* on your keyboard as a shortcut.

When the presets library is opened, you will see that it is divided into two sections: a tree view in the left column, showing all the materials organized by type, so that you can browse the one you need; and another column on the right showing thumbnails of every material of the category you're in.

When you find the right material for your object, simply drag the thumbnail you want from the right column to the material shown in your shader tree, or you can directly drag it into the viewport, letting it drop on the object The material will be automatically applied. There are other types of presets too that can be found on the Luxology Share Site `http://www.luxology.com/asset/`.

Manual creation of a material

If you decide to manually create your material, you must use the **Properties** panel. In the **Shader Tree** field, click on the material's name to see its properties. You will find the following:

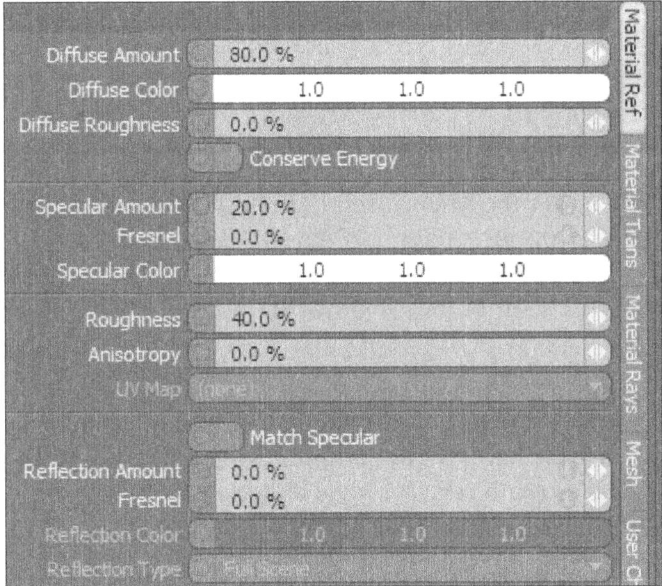

In that panel, you will find everything you need to set up a material. Let's see what parameters we need for each type:

- **Diffuse Color**: This decides the color of the material. Just click on it and choose a color from the color picker window.
- **Conserve Energy**: I recommend to have this box checked, in order to get more natural results when working with reflective or specular materials.
- **Specular Amount**: This decides how much light the material will reflect. A value higher than zero will increase the specular highlights on your material.
- **Reflection Amount**: This decides the intensity of the reflections on the material. The higher the number, the more will it reflect the environment and other objects.
- **Double Sided**: Check this box if you want your material to be visible both from the front and back as well. This is useful when you have to deal with very thin objects such as paper or curtains, to avoid the need of giving them some thickness, thus increasing the number of polygons.

These properties are under the **Material Ref** tab (look to the right of the **Properties** panel). There is an extra option under the **Material Trans** tab. If you click on that tab, you will find a **Luminous Intensity** field. Give it a value higher than zero to make your material emit light in order to get an emitter.

Using textures

The use of textures is a basic technique for mimicking real world materials. The textures allow us to create very complex materials in an easy and quick way just by faking them with images pasted on the surface.

Imagine a wall of bricks. You could create the wall by modeling every brick, adding mortar, and layering on every small detail, but that would take forever. It would be easier to take a photo of a brick wall or paint a texture to create that look.

Types of projection

modo, and every other 3D software in the market, uses an axis-based projection system to stamp textures on your objects. You can imagine a texture moving along one of the three axes, approaching the object until finally meeting it. This technique is simpler than it seems. There are many types of projections present depending on the topology of the mesh. Now, we will learn which projection will be good for our model.

Planar projection

What you see in the following figure is an example of a planar projection:

First, I generated a cube primitive. Then, I selected one of its faces and assigned a material to it. Thereafter, I loaded an image for it in the shader tree and set the **Projection Type** to **Planar**.

Do you see the small coordinates icon at the bottom left of the image? It shows the general orientation of the x, y, and z dimensions in the 3D environment. You can see that the textured face is facing the x axis, so that's the axis appropriate for this particular case as a planar projection.

To let you know how it works more deeply, let me perform a small experiment. What if we do the same with a sphere? Let's have a look:

Did you see how the image gets distorted? This is because a planar projection works best on a planar surface, where all of its area is completely facing an axis. That's why it's important to choose the right projection type for each object.

Cubic projection

So, we know how to project a texture on a face. But what if I want to texture the six faces of the cube? Now, we will be using a brick texture to make it clearer. Let's load a brick wall image using a planar projection and see what happens:

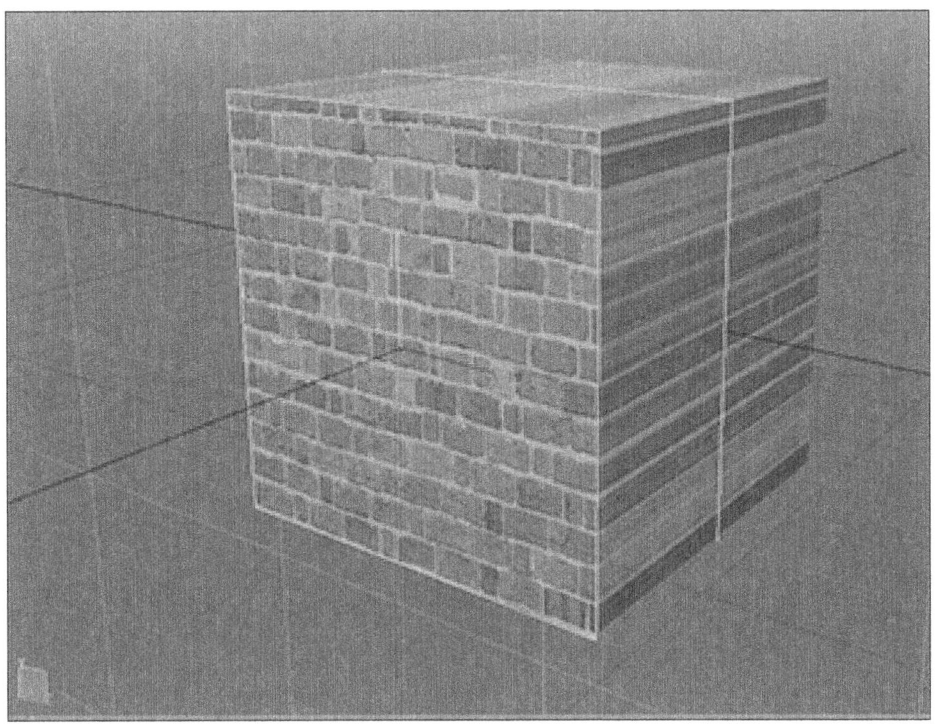

You guessed it right: it doesn't work. See how the texture gets extremely distorted in every face not facing the x axis. Now, it's clear that the planar projection is only good when we want it on a surface facing only one axis. The correct projection for this case will be cubic as shown in the following figure:

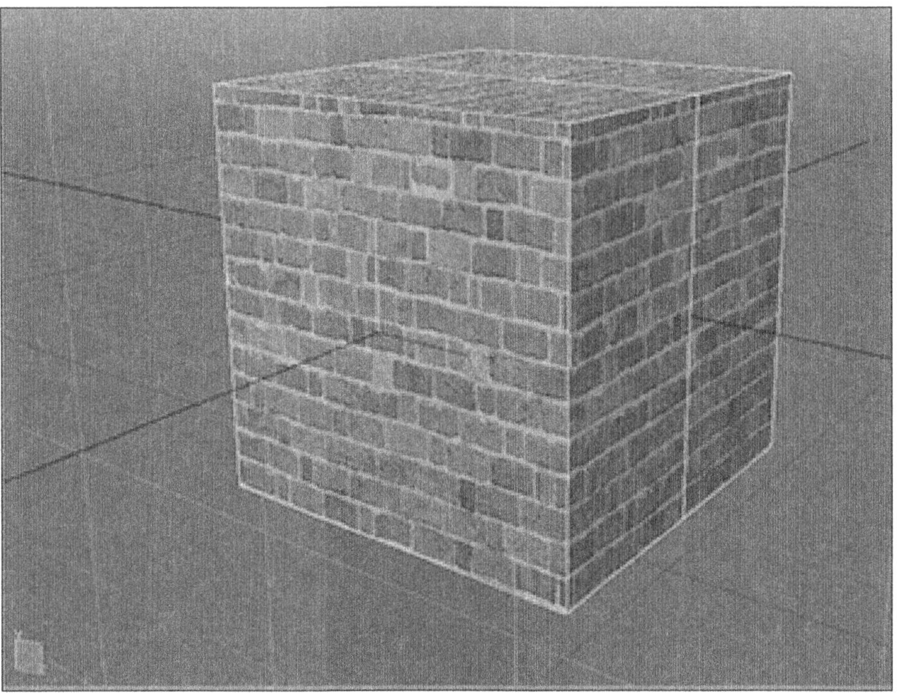

What the cubic projection does is estimate the axis each face is aligned to. Then, it planar projects the texture onto that face based on the axis it thinks it's most aligned to.

Spherical projection

Let's get something more difficult: a sphere.

In a polygonal world, like the one we are working on now, there are no spheres really. A sphere in a 3D software is a geometric body with hundreds and thousands of faces, enough to give the illusion of being a curved surface. So, we will have a high number of faces, each facing a different direction. The solution for this is as simple as changing the projection to spherical.

A typical example would be texturing a planet. If you search the Internet, you will find several textures of planets available to download, such as the following figure representing the planet Jupiter (beautiful, isn't it?):

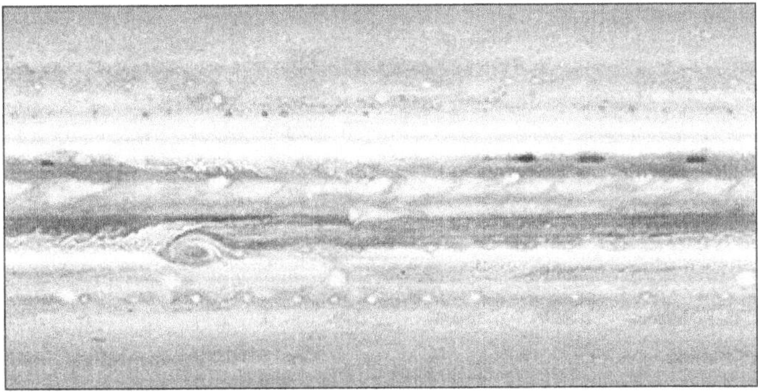

So, if we project this texture over a sphere with a spherical projection, the result will be as shown in the following figure:

There you go. The image wraps around the sphere perfectly with no distortion at all.

UV mapping

There will be situations when the projection methods explained just won't work because of the complexity of the model. In such situations, you will need to manually set up the mesh with a custom projection type known as UV mapping.

As an example, generate a teapot primitive (**Geometry** | **Unit Primitives** | **In Current Mesh** | **Teapot**) and switch to the **UV** tab. You will see the workspace divided into two viewports: one being a simple perspective view and the other showing the UV space for that object.

In the UV viewport, you can see how a typical UV map looks like. It shows different parts of the model unfolded in a 2D space, such that you can later project a planar texture over it.

Do you remember your school days, when you had to cut a cardboard in the shape of an unwrapped cube? That's exactly how UV mapping works. You take the geometry you want to unfold and then project it in the UV space, as if it were a cardboard.

There are several tools and techniques for UV mapping an object, but for now being a beginner, just keep in mind the foundations of this technique for a more advanced stage.

Anyways, if you understood how UV mapping works and want to give it a try, I would recommend that you use an automatic unfold action named **UV Projection Tool**, which is located at the top of the UV mapping toolbox:

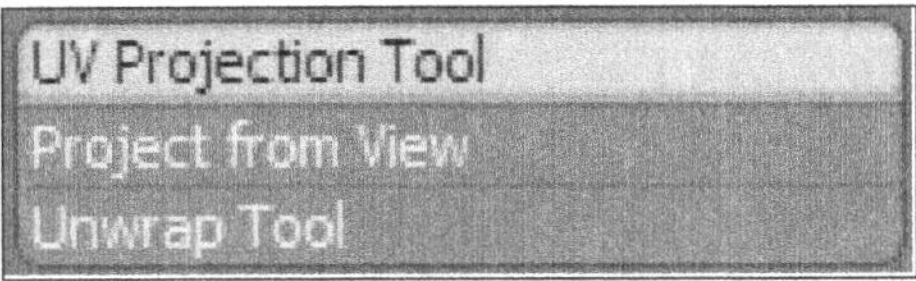

Then in the tool's properties, just set the **Projection Type** mode to **Atlas** and click on **OK**. The object will be unfolded in the UV space automatically. From then, you can apply any texture that will be displayed on your object according to the UV map generated.

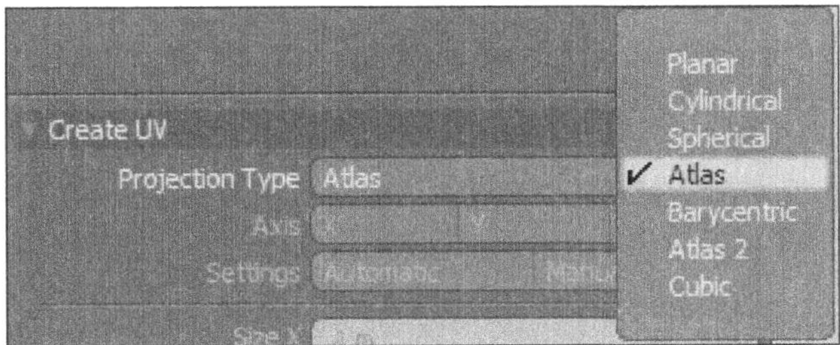

How to apply textures

Now that we know the different basic types of projection, we should also know the procedure to apply them. The first few steps are always the same, regardless of the projection type.

First of all, with your selections done and your material assigned and named, we must locate it in the shader tree. It will be automatically displayed, showing its name and the material item linked to it. In the following figure, I have created a material called **my material** which is shown in the **Shader Tree** field (expanded):

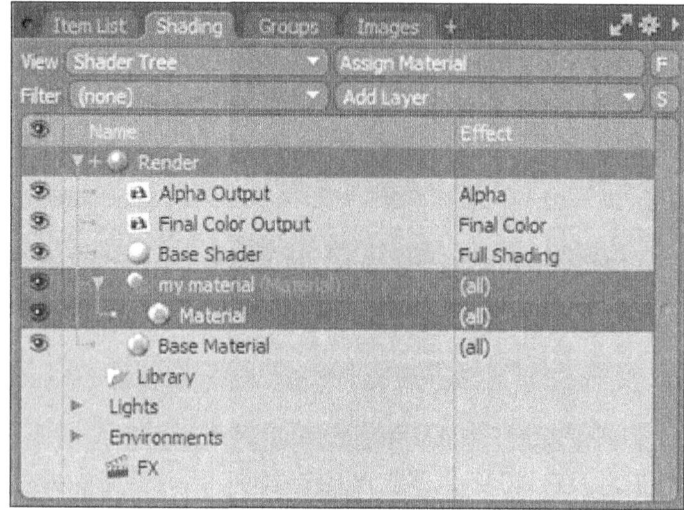

Notice how the last material you create gets automatically selected. The next step will be loading an image for it. To do that, click on the **Add Layer** button and choose **Image Map | (load image)**. A regular file browser will pop up to let you choose your image file:

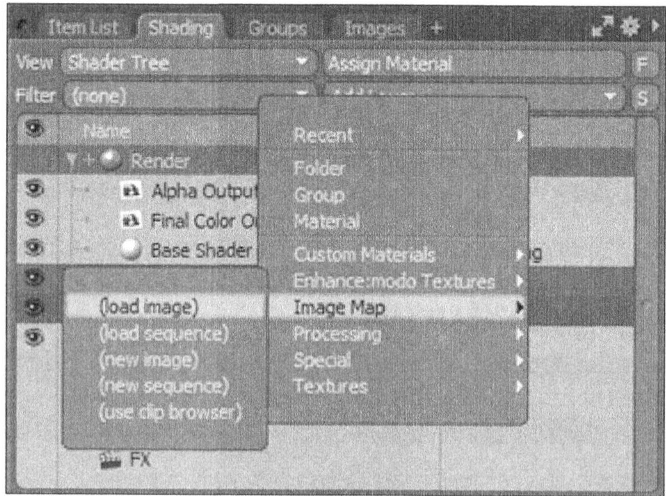

Now that we have our image loaded, we can decide which kind of projection we want. To do this, we will select the image texture element and then go to the **Texture Locator** tab in the **Properties** panel:

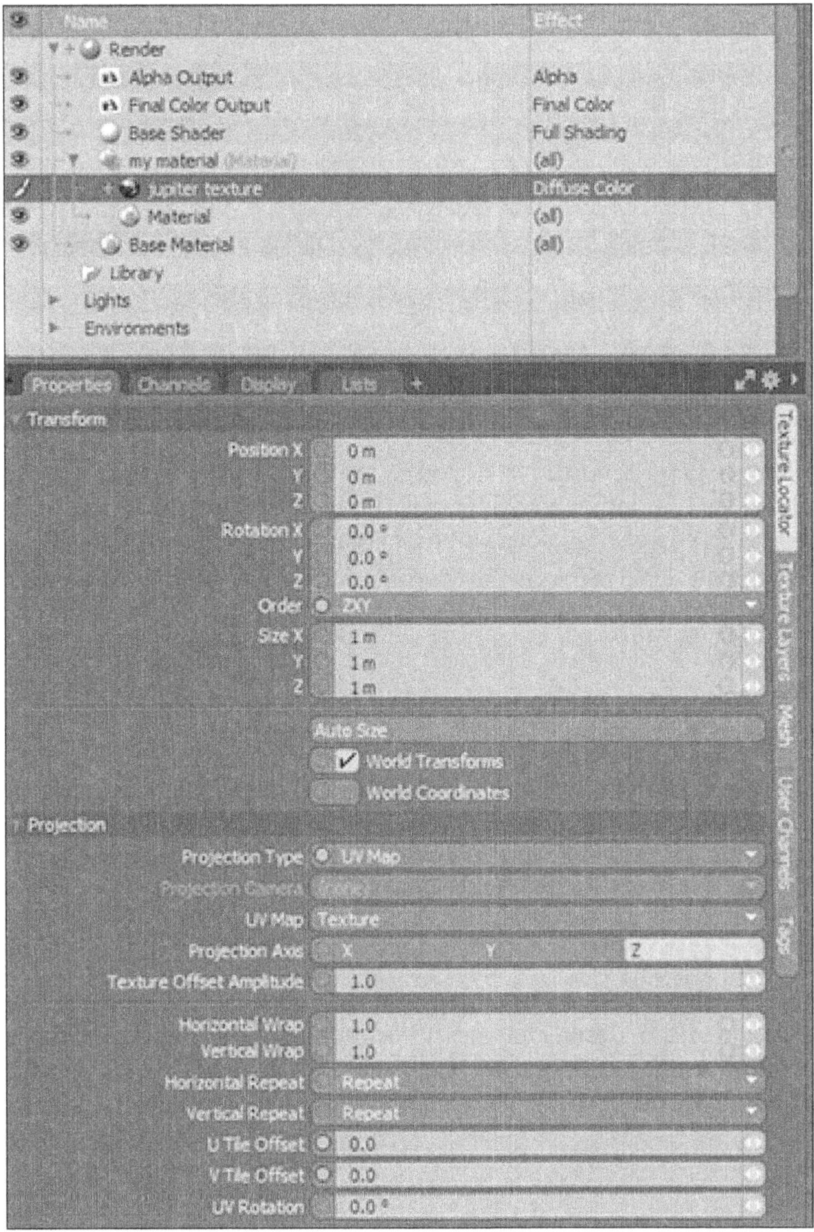

You must now check the **Projection Type** drop-down menu to choose the type of projection you want. We are working with a sphere, so will choose **Spherical**:

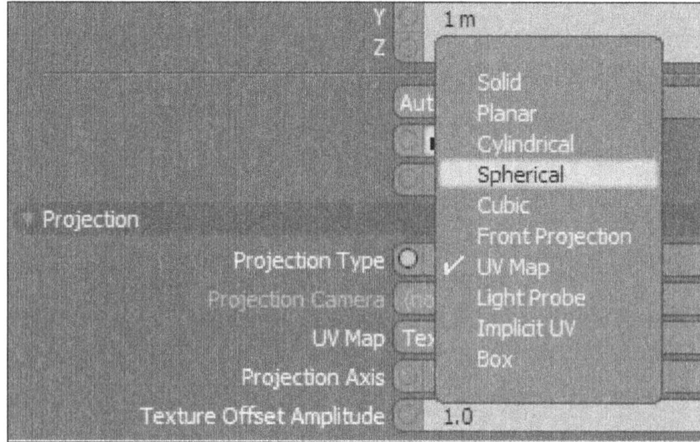

One more thing to have in mind is that you can tweak the position of the textures, as well as their size or rotation across an axis. The **Transform** section in the **Texture Locator** tab will let you change your values, in case you want to move, scale, or rotate the texture. Another useful tool I use a lot is the **Auto Size** button, which automatically assigns a size to the texture in order to enable it to fit the model. You decide if you want an automatic sizing of the textures or manually scale, rotate, or move it.

Special effects

In addition to the basic features of each type of material, there are a bunch of tricks you can use to successfully mimic real world materials at ease. We will focus on the basics of these special features to get better and more realistic materials in an easy way.

Bump mapping

In the real world, there will be lots of materials that show some roughness. In fact, most of the real world materials have that bumpiness in some degree. Only very flat surfaces such as mirrors will not show bumps at all. There is a way to get this effect inside modo without generating a dense geometry.

In the previous screenshot, you can see how bump mapping can affect the look of a material. The two cubes are assigned to the same material, but the one on the right has a bump map effect attached, showing the roughness that makes it more realistic and better looking. The one on the left is only a cube with a rust texture and looks polished because there is no bump mapping at all.

Applying bump mapping

In order to create this effect over a texture, you must locate the material you want the bump mapping for, in the shader tree. If you expand the material (by clicking on the little arrow next to its name), you will see two items inside it: a material item and a texture item:

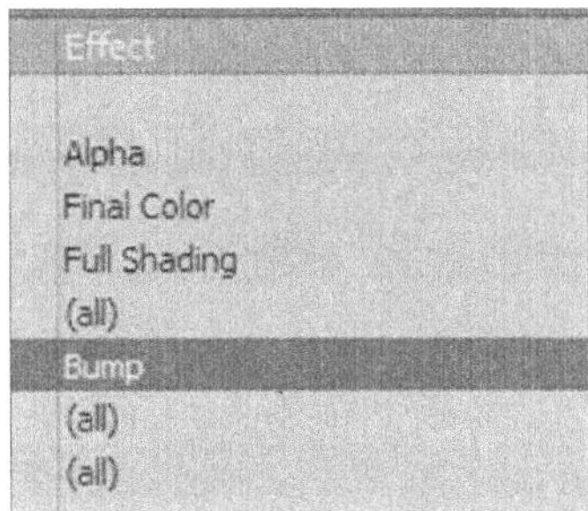

In the right-hand side column, next to the texture, you can see the mode the texture is working in, on the material. This column is named as **Effect**. By default, this mode is set to **Diffuse Color**, meaning that the texture will be shown as a regular image covering the material. Carry out the following steps:

- Right-click on the texture item. You will see a pop-up menu with some options. Click on **Duplicate** to generate a copy of that texture inside the material.
- In the **Effect** column, right click on the **Diffuse Color** attribute to change it. Look for **Bump** under **Surface Shading**.

Now, you have your material configured with a texture as diffuse and the same texture as bumpiness, what we call a bump map. If you find the bump map is too strong for your material, you can always lower its intensity in the **Properties** panel for that item, lowering the opacity of that particular layer, or else changing the **Bump Amplitude** value on the material itself.

Transparencies

Transparencies, or Alpha mapping are a very common technique you will need to take into account, if you want to save some work and not make your models unnecessarily complex. Let's see how:

There will be situations where you can solve complex shapes by using transparencies, without needing to create a complex model. Think about a leaf on a tree from the perspective of a 3D artist. It's basically a slightly distorted plane with the texture of a leaf on a planar projection, leaving the rest as transparency. We call this technique alpha mapping.

Applying alpha mapping

First of all, you need to have your texture in an image format that supports alpha channel. This can be PNG, TIFF, TGA or whatever you feel more comfortable with. Usually, PNGs are recommended in most 3D software. Check that your image contains transparency by opening it in Photoshop. Follow this procedure to get alpha mapping:

- Apply the texture in your material as usual.
- Check the properties of the texture item in the shader tree. At the bottom of the panel, you will see an option called **Alpha Channel**. Make sure it's set to **Use**.
- In the **Effect** column, change the mode of the texture item (right-click on it) from **Diffuse Color** (by default) to **RGBA**. You will find this mode under the **Special Effects** option.

By doing this, you are telling modo that an image should be applied as diffuse using its RGB (red, green, blue) values, along with using the A value (which stands for alpha) as a transparency.

Transparencies can also be set by using a greyscale image where black is considered fully transparent and white fully opaque. This can be set to **Transparent Amount** and will create the same effect.

If you did as indicated, you will end up with a material that looks like the one in the previous figure.

Specular maps

Specular mapping is a useful technique to get more natural and realistic results when working with reflective materials. Look at the following figure:

It's a very simple material: just a plane with a wooden floor applied in a planar projection. I wanted to represent a reflective floor, so raised the value in the reflection box of the material. You can see that the floor is reflecting. But you shouldn't be happy with this result, as it looks pretty ugly and amateurish. Let's see how we can enhance it.

We will need a specular map, which is a texture controlling the amount of reflectiveness of the material. To do this, perform the same operation as always: duplicate the texture item and change its mode. In this case, we will want the **Reflection Amount** effect, located under the option **Basic Channels**. See the difference:

I have split the same object into two halves: the left half is the original state, while the right half shows the same material, but with a specular map added. Notice how the reflections get way more natural by using the specular amount mode.

What modo does is take the image and convert it (internally) to a black and white image, where darker tones mean lesser reflection and brighter tones mean more reflection. That way, you can see no reflections (or weaker ones) in darker areas, instead of letting the reflections cover the surface entirely.

Fresnel

Fresnel is a physical feature of reflective materials related to the angle of incidence of reflection. Let's clarify this a little. Look at the following figure:

Let's say we are told to create a porcelain material. It seems to be an easy task as we just need to make a white material and give it some reflections, right? No, you are wrong. See how a material with a 25% reflection value looks as has been shown in the previous figure. It doesn't work at all and that is because a teapot is a curvy surface.

In the real world, curvy surfaces show an effect called Fresnel. This means that, for a curvy surface, the reflections tend to populate the sides of the object more (from the perspective of the viewer) than in the front (areas facing the viewer perpendicularly). It's a very interesting effect because it's dynamic, meaning that the reflections move to the silhouette of the object as you change your view, for example, move around it. Let's see how to get this nice effect.

Tweaking reflection/fresnel properties

Knowing that the fresnel effect divides the reflections into front and side (from the perspective of the viewer), modo gives us two fields that you can tweak in order to control this division. Locate these fields in the material's **Properties** panel:

These two fields control the front reflections by using the **Reflection Amount** value, and the side reflections with the **Fresnel** value. As I said before, we want a material similar to porcelain and so should do the following:

- Set the **Fresnel** effect to **100%**. You can tweak this value to fit your likings. We will be using 100% fresnel value to see the effects more clearly.
- Set the **Reflection Amount** value to something very low. Try 1%.

With these values, you will get the following material:

Now we have something way better. See how strong the reflections are in the silhouette (controlled by the **Fresnel** value) and how soft and subtle they are in the rest (controlled by the **Reflection Amount** value), acting, as a fresnel would work in the real world. Always try to use this technique when dealing with curvy reflective materials.

Summary

By the end of this chapter we have learned how to recreate real world materials by using different kinds of materials inside modo, how to apply textures and project them on the objects, and also some extra methods and tricks for more complex models.

In the next chapter, we will cover different methods and techniques to illuminate your scene, as well as dig into some workflows to add a nice mood to your render by using the lights.

4
Illuminating a Scene

In this chapter we will cover the main aspects of illuminating a scene. You will learn the different types of light, and how/when to use them, along with some tips to get a good illumination according to your scene.

Our main concerns will be the following:

- Working with lights
- Types of light
- Illuminating a scene
- Tips on lighting

Working with lights

Before starting to explain about lights, we need to learn how to create and manipulate them. Once you know how to handle them, you will be ready to start learning the who-is-who in the lightning stage. Let's start with the basics.

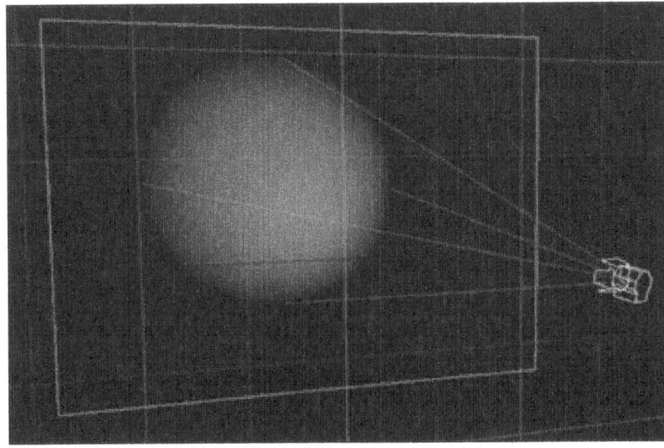

Adding a light

Lights are handled in modo just like regular items. You can move, rotate, and scale them, and of course, tweak their properties.

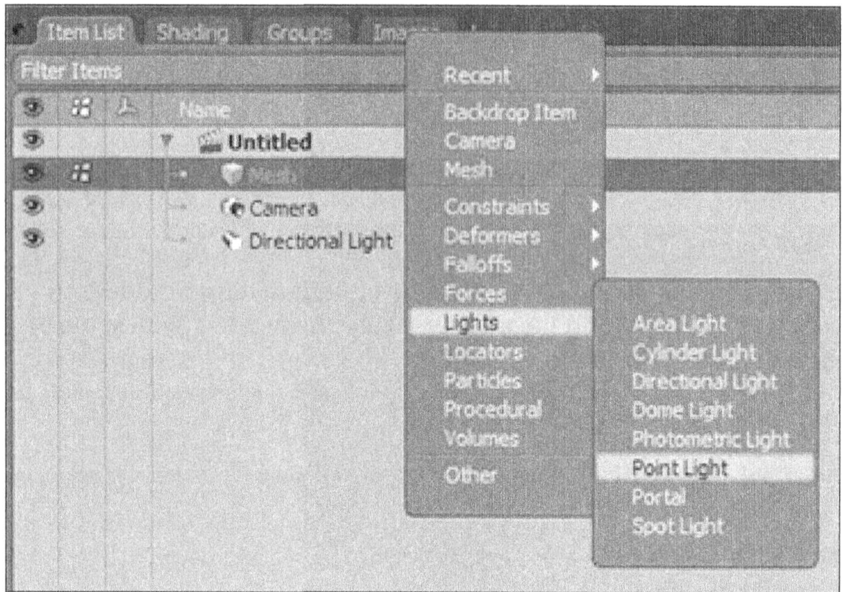

By default, a newly created scene has got a default light already. You can use it, change its type, or add as many as you need. In order to add a new light you should go to the **Item List** tab, and then click on the **Add Item** button. In the drop-down menu go to **Lights**, then choose the type of light you want.

The other way to do this is by using the top menu. Navigate to **Item** | **Create Light** and choose the type you want.

Setting the type of a light

You can always change the type of the light just created (or change an existent light). In the **Item List** tab, right-click the light you want to change, and from the menu click on **Change Type**, then choose the type you want for your light.

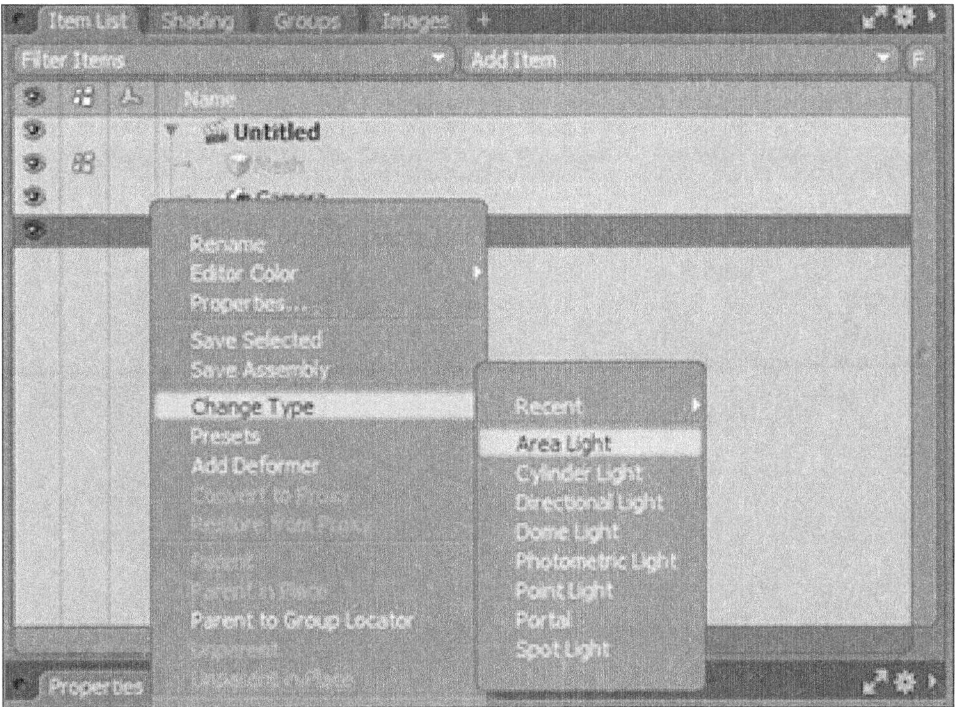

Placing lights

As said previously, lights are like all other regular items. So you can move, rotate, and scale them as you need. You will have the following two ways of placing a light:

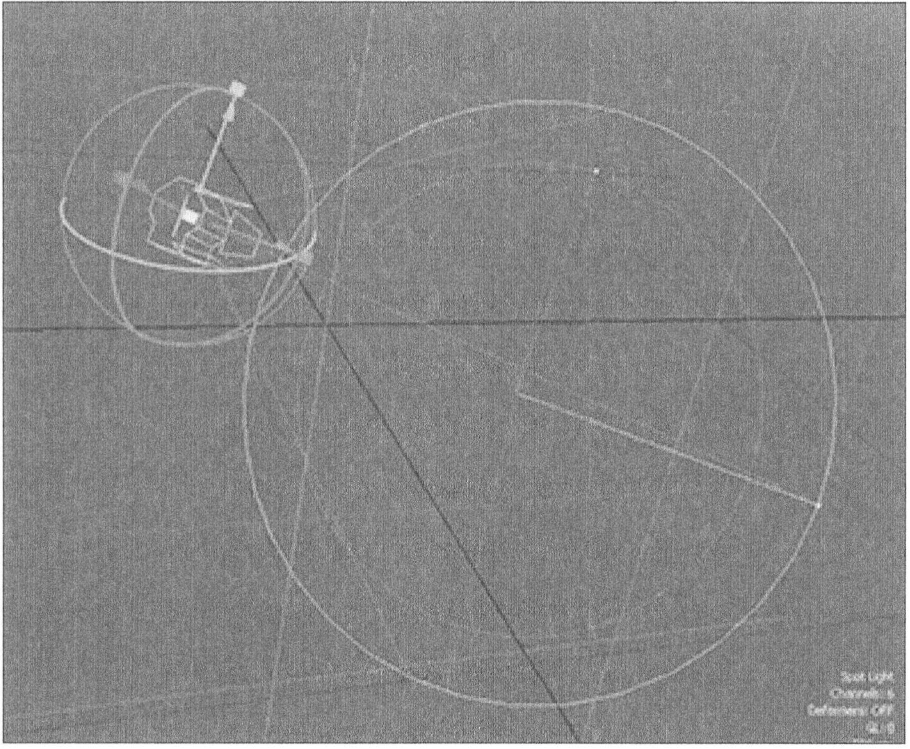

- **Direct manipulation**: Working in item mode, click on the light on any of the viewports—or directly in the **Item List** tab— and use the corresponding tools (*W* for moving, *R* for scaling, or *Y* for rotating).
- **Subjective manipulation**: A more interesting and practical way to move a light is by changing the viewport to light view mode. Once you change it, your view will be literally inside the light, so the direction you are facing will be the direction of the light. In this view, use your standard viewport controls to orientate the light.

Enabling/disabling lights

Usually, there are occasions when you need to turn off a light, or a number of them. The first thought would be turning its intensity value to zero, but there is a more practical way to temporarily disable a light.

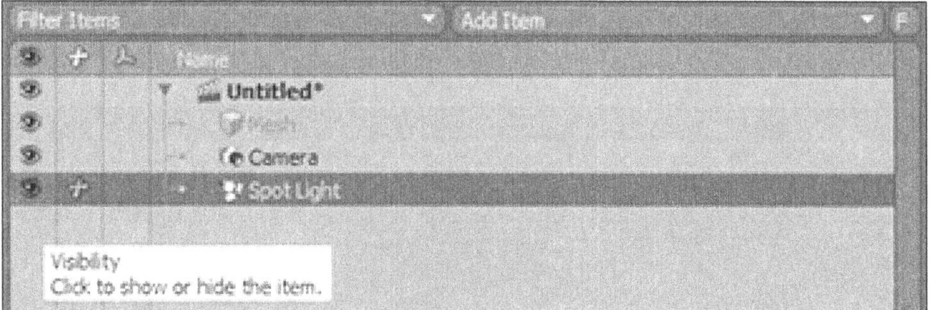

If you take a look at the items list, you will see a column on the left of the panel showing a little eye icon. That column shows the visibility state of each item. The eye means that it's visible, and you can click on that icon to totally disable the light (or any item, in fact), and click on it again to enable it back.

Of course you can do rest of the basic operations with the lights, as with other kinds of items including enabling/disabling them, grouping them in a single folder, and so on.

Types of light

Now that you know the basic operations you can do with the lights and how to handle them, let's take a look at the different kinds of lights you can work with. This will not be an in-depth guide of each type, but a recommended list of what types of lights will be more useful to you in order to work in a real scene, along with some recommendations about when and how to use each of them.

Spot Light

A Spot Light works as a torch, meaning the light coming from it travels in the shape of a cone. This kind of light will light everything that comes inside the cone, leaving the rest unlit.

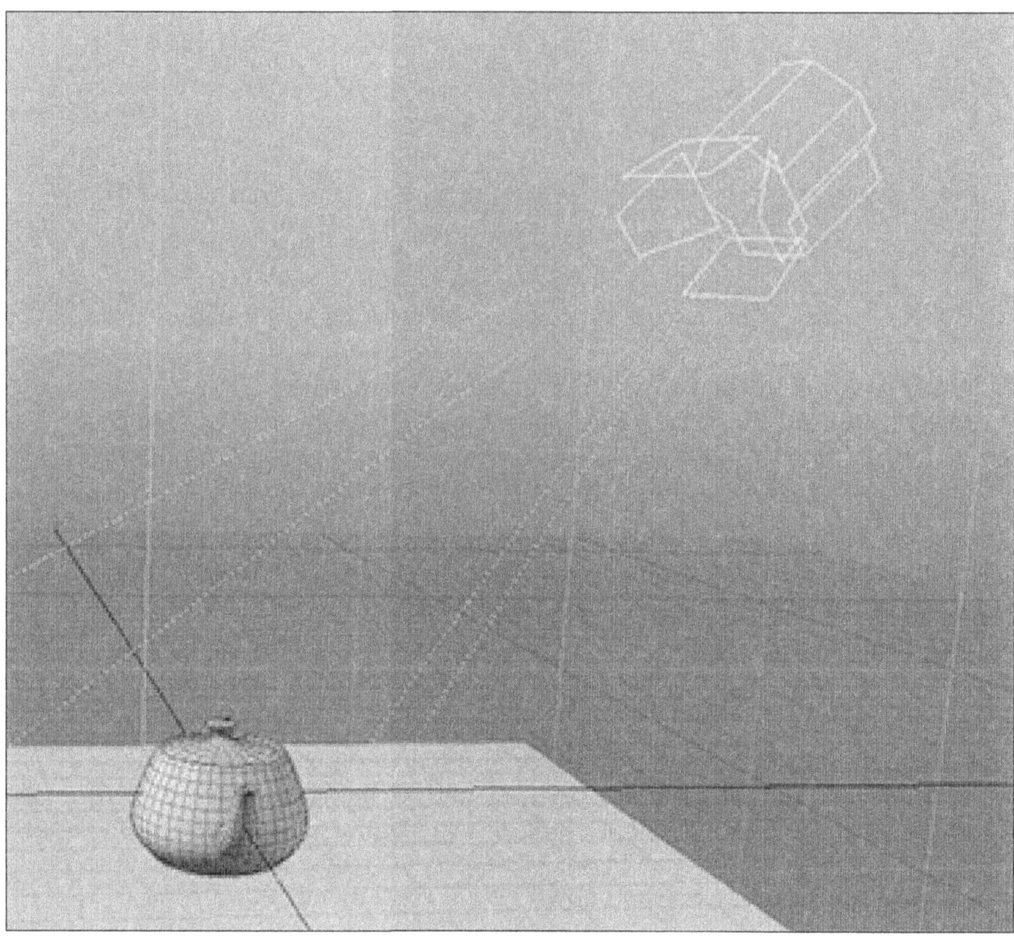

It's got its own properties panel—as with every item in modo—where you can tweak various aspects. The panel for **Spot Light** looks like the following screenshot:

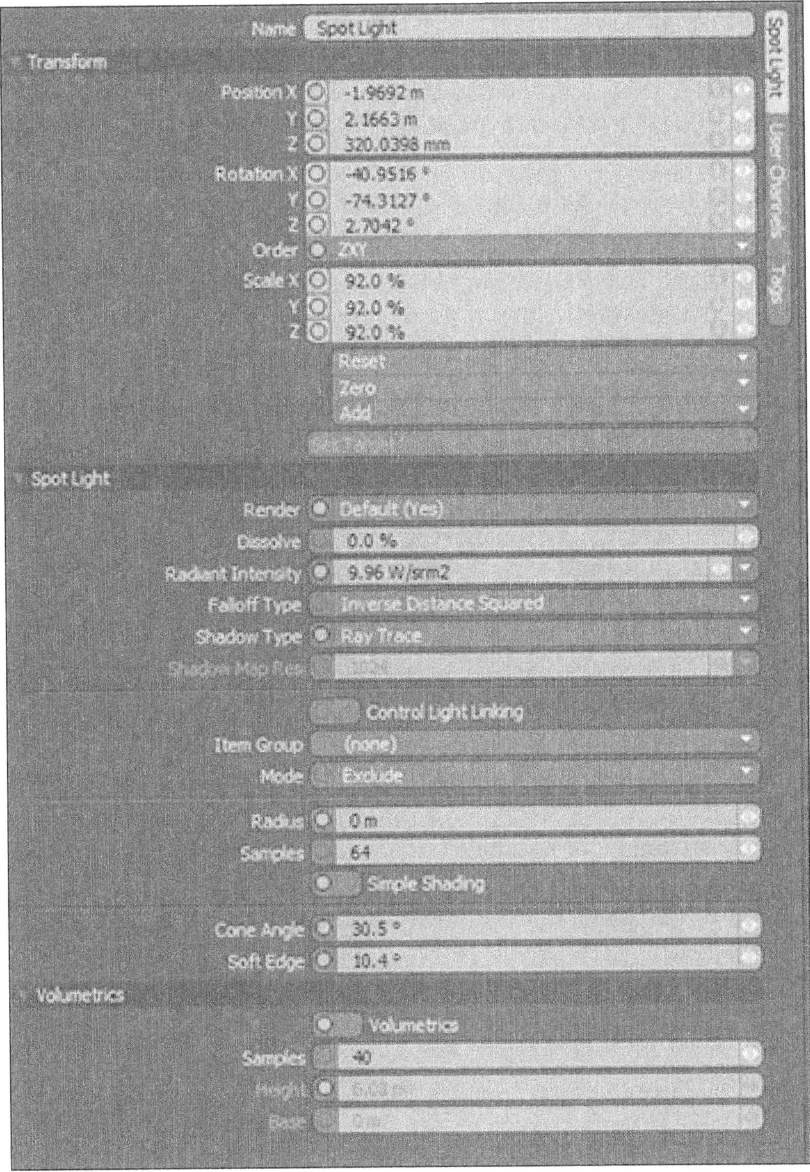

There are plenty of options, but for a beginner, you should look at the following basic settings:

- **Radiant Intensity**: This is the power of the light source. The greater the intensity, the more powerful will be the light.
- **Cone Angle**: This controls how big the base of the cone is. With a low number, you will get a narrow lit area, while it gets bigger as you raise this value.
- **Soft Edge**: Leave it set to zero if you want totally sharp edges of the lit area. Increase it to make that area blurry.
- **Volumetrics**: Enable the **Volumetrics** checkbox to get a nice "God's rays" effect, as if you were casting light through fog. You can then tweak the height value to make the effect more or less strong.

The following figure will show you how different settings create different effects:

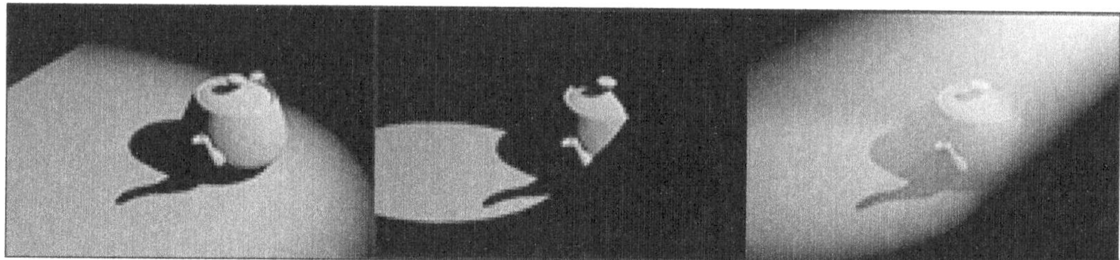

From left to right:

- Wide cone angle, soft edges
- Narrow cone angle, hard edges
- **Volumetrics** enabled

Point light

Point lights act as bulbs. Think of them as spheres casting light in all directions. Due to their own nature, they cannot be oriented in any way, only positioned. You will recognize them by the particular shape of the shadows they generate. Look at the following figure:

I have put a point light in the center of a group of teapots. It casts light to all directions, so the shadows all converge to the same point, where the light is. The use of it will be, obviously, creating light bulbs.

The settings available for this kind of lights is the same as that for the Spot Lights (of course, no cone angle, fuzzy edges, and so on). You can tweak its intensity, color, and Volumetrics in the same way.

Area light

Area lights are a bit more advanced lights. They can generate what we call **diffuse lightning**. This means they generate shadows that soften in a very natural way, making them perfect to mimic indirect light, avoiding that sharp look from the rest of the light.

They are square-shaped panels that emit light. So you can control the size of the panel to make them cover a larger area.

The following figure shows the nice shadow effect you can generate with these kind of lights:

The area lights are a perfect solution to place in a window, if you want to simulate indirect light coming from outside. It's important to take a look at one important property of it, which is samples.

The samples value controls the quality of the light. The fewer the samples, the more noisy will be the shadows. If you increase the samples, you will get finer and cleaner shadows, but it will take more time to render. Find the right balance for your scene. The following figure shows the difference:

The figure on the left was rendered with a value of 5 samples. It took 4 seconds. That's fast, but with a very noisy result.

The figure on the right shows a value of 500 samples, so it's got really fine shadows, but it took 20 seconds to render. That's 5 times slower. The general advice is that you increase your samples till you don't get visible noise in the render.

Cylinder light

I personally love cylinder lights. These kind of lights emit a very particular illumination, making them really useful to mimic fluorescent tubes.

We could say that cylinder lights are an area version of the point lights in some way. They are shaped like a tube, so they cast light from a cylinder in all directions. The effect will be like placing a point light, but emitting diffuse lightning.

In the following figure, there is a cylinder light placed in the center of the teapots group. See how the shadows converge like with a point light, but with that soft and nice shading of the area light.

As for the area lights, you can control the amount of samples to balance the result correctly. Remember, more samples means finer shadows, but a longer render time.

Portals

When dealing with interior scenes, portals are a great tool to help the light do its work more efficiently.

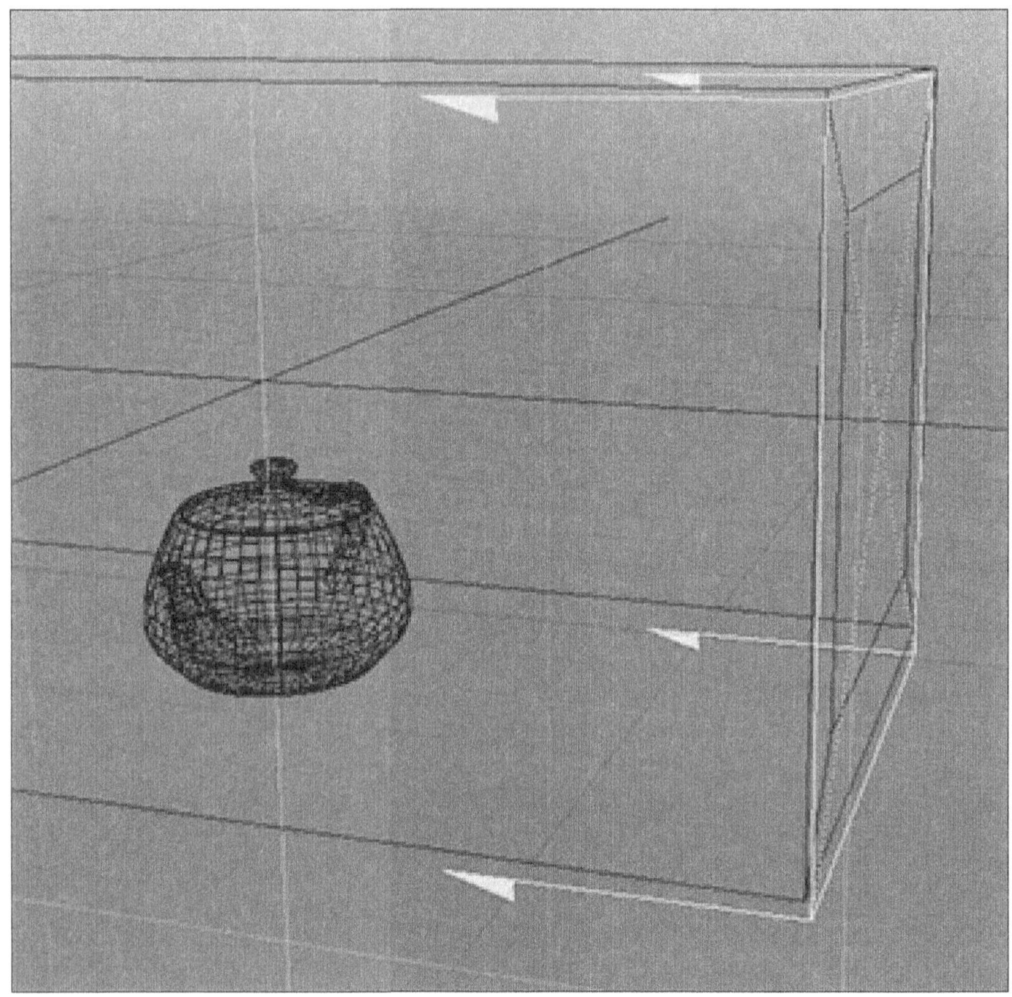

In short, a portal is a photon magnet. This means that, what a portal does, is that it attracts the greatest amount of light possible around it, and casts it through itself in one direction. The following figure shows how you can benefit from a portal, using the scene in the previous figure:

I have rendered the same scene at a very low quality, so you can see the differences. The top figure shows the result of opening a hole in a wall (as if it were a window) and allowing the outside light to come into the room. You can notice how noisy the result is. That's because it's very hard for the light to reach the interior of the room. And this is when portals show their potential.

In the bottom figure, I have placed a portal in the window. With the exact settings, you can see how the results are way better, even at a low sample setup. The portal is attracting the outside light and casting it directly into the room. That's how you can benefit from the portals in a practical situation.

You may think about the differences between using a portal and using an area light. Why don't you just put an area light to make that work? The answer is about effectiveness.

If you use an area light, you will have to set up an intensity value for it, and also a color to make it match the outside light. On the other hand, portals are automatic. So, you place a portal, and automatically it will get the same intensity and color of the outside. Just place it, and let it do its work. An area light will do the same thing, but you will have to set it up, so portals will ease your life, as compared to area lights.

Illuminating a scene

Knowing the different kind of lights, now we are able to decide which kind of lights we will need, depending on whether we want to simulate indirect light from the outside, a light bulb in the ceiling, a fluorescent in the wall, and so on.

Once you have placed your lights in the proper position, and adjusted their intensity and color, you will want to have a clear idea of what your render will look like. Years ago, this task was very tedious and time consuming, but now we have the option of having a low quality render, that you can use as a preview of the final image in real time. Let´s take a look at the different options available to use the preview window.

Working with previews

Inside modo, you have what we call a **Preview** window, which is a floating window, showing your render in a very fast way, without the need to render the entire scene with full quality, thus saving a substantial amount of time.

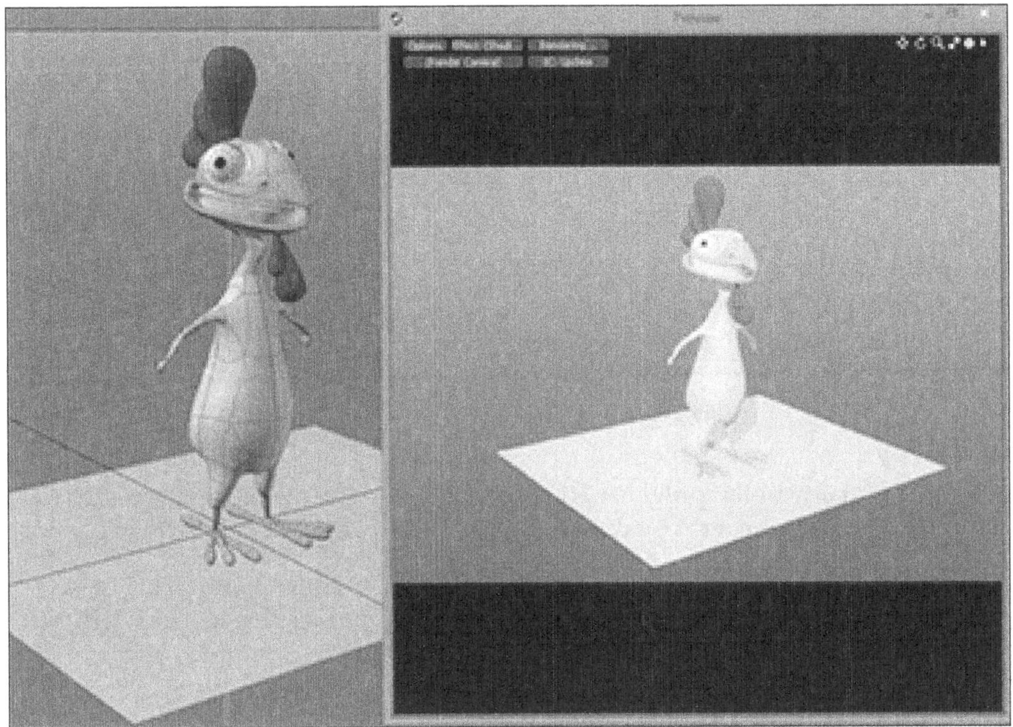

Have in mind that the **Preview** window will show the result of the camera view, so you will have to first place the camera, then launch the **Preview** window. It is available from the **Render** | **Open preview** render, or by pressing *F8* on your keyboard.

You can keep your **Preview** window open while working, so if you move your camera, change something in the scene, move objects, and so on, it will be reflected in the preview, giving a constant real-time approach of what your final render will look like.

Preview modes

In the upper-left corner of the **Preview** window you will see a button called **Options**. If you click on it, a drop-down menu will appear with many options you can choose to set up the preview. We will focus on two of the options, **Quality** and **Full Resolution**.

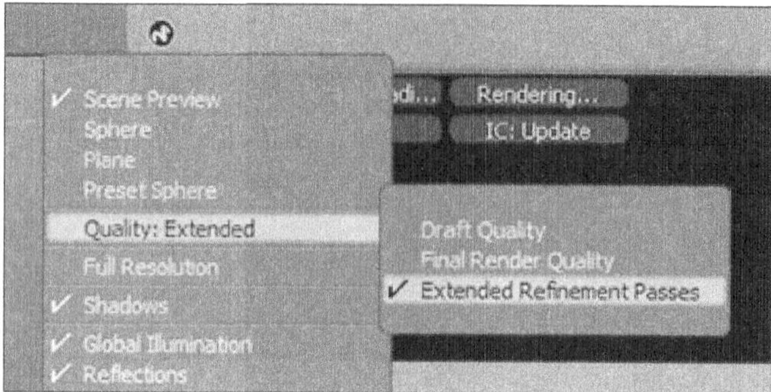

Quality

This sets the quality of the preview. The higher the quality, the more precise the preview will be, but slower. You can choose the following three different levels:

- **Draft Quality**: This shows a preview with a very little quality. This is not suitable as an approach to the final render, but it's fine to check light intensities, general setup, and so on.
- **Final Render Quality**: This makes a preview with the settings stated for your scene. The preview will show the same quality of the final render, but it's still not suitable as a final render itself.
- **Extended Refinement Passes**: This one is a bit more advanced preview mode. What it does, is calculate pass after pass, to refine the image more and more, even over passing the settings on your scene. It will continue refining the preview forever, until you stop it. This mode is suitable for a final render. Just launch an Extended preview, and let it work. Eventually it will reach a level of refinement suitable to use as a final image.

Full Resolution

The **Full Resolution** option must be checked if you want your preview the same size as your final render. If it's not checked, the preview will be resized to fit the area of the **Preview** window. It's good to have it enabled if you want to use an Extended preview as a final render.

The RayGL view

There is a second option to have a preview of your scene. It´s a bit different than the **Preview** window, since it shows it directly into the visor, regardless of the view you're using, so you will not have to use the camera view if you don't want to.

The RayGL view also shows the preview preserving the wireframe view, so you will be able to check the shading and illumination of your scene, and the topology of it at the same time, but always with a very low quality.

You have the following two options for it:

- **Fast**: The preview will show just a basic approach of the render. Basically just lights and shadows, so you can have a quick look at the overall setup.
- **Full**: The preview shows everything, including indirect lights, and all the extended features.

To enable it, click on the **Ray GL** button located in the upper-left corner of every visor. In the drop-down menu, choose the option you want for it (**Full** or **Fast**).

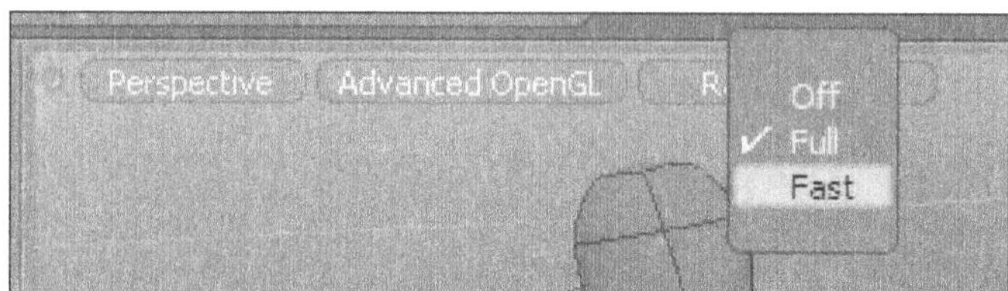

Cool and warm

We will now focus on the principles of colors of light. Choosing the color of a light is always important, since they will give us different kind of moods in the scene, and will re-create different kind of light sources, depending if we're working with sunlight, fluorescent, incandescent, and so on.

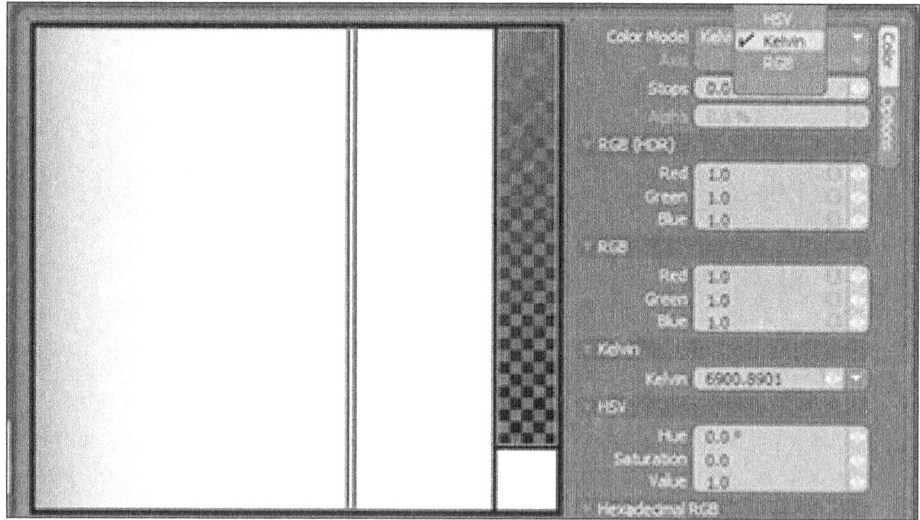

First of all you need to know how to change the color of a light. As for every other item, the lights have their own properties panel where you can control all the values available. In the **Shading** panel, **Item List** tab, you can click on the light you want to change, then in the properties panel, go to the Texture layer tab where you will see a clickable field labeled as **Color**. Click on that field, and you will see a panel like the one shown in the preceding screenshot.

Inside that panel you can choose between three different kind of color modes. Since we are working with colors of light, we must choose the **Kelvin** mode, which is a color picker based on the light's temperature.

So, how do we choose the right color? The Kelvin color picker shows only a gradation from red to blue. And that's the only option available for this palette. Lights can be warm (more reddish), or can be cool (more bluish). My advice is that you use a Kelvin table to decide the color of your light, depending on its nature. There are plenty of Kelvin tables available online. The following figure shows one of them, taken from `http://university.maxlite.com`:

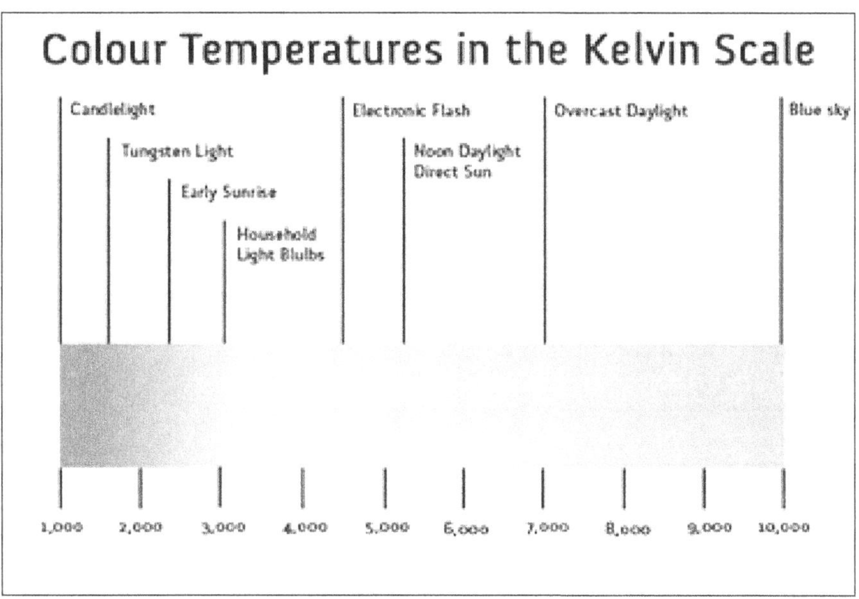

As you see, it's easy to choose the correct Kelvin value for your light, if you know what kind of light it will be. Also, you don't have to eyeball the color on your palette, of course. Just fill the Kelvin field with the number indicated and it's done.

Having some color variation in the lights is always a good advice to enrich the look of your scene.

Key lights

When lightning a scene, it is important to know some rules about positioning the lights for the shot. Different colors will give you different moods, and the positioning will contribute the scene, revealing details or making it more interesting. We will now discuss a classical three point lightning, which will make you understand the basics of using lights. So, let's begin with the key light.

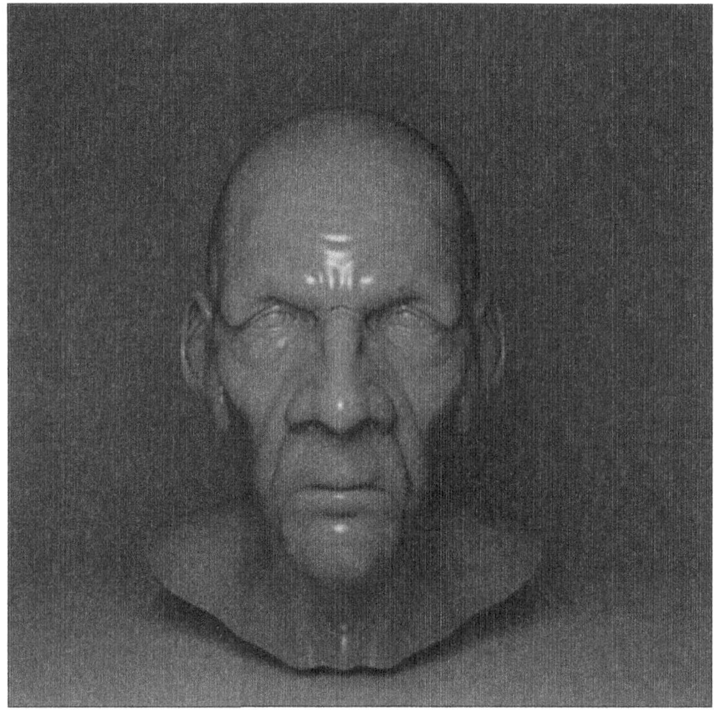

What you see in the preceding figure is an object taken from the presets library, and a standard studio background. The illumination here is very basic, since there is only one light in the scene.

I chose an area light to use it as key light, because of its diffuse nature, casting very soft shadows and also giving an interesting shading of the volumes.

The mission of the key light is to point directly at the object you want to light, showing its general shape and volume, so it's better to set a white color to it, so it shows the object in a neutral way.

So, now that we have our key light, let's move on to the next stage.

Fill lights

The next step will be setting the fill lights. Once the key light is done, there are usually areas that are not covered, typically behind the object. That causes it to blend somehow with the background, losing the silhouette of it, and in some way making it to look not well defined.

That's the point of creating fill lights, while not contributing directly to the shading of the object, they in fact state a separation between the object and the background, adding information to the image, and giving it a more deeper look.

I also gave it a warm color to give it a more pleasant background.

Contours

This third stage of the illumination is a very interesting phase. In the previous stages, I have put soft lights to get a nice pleasant atmosphere. Now we're going to go in the opposite direction.

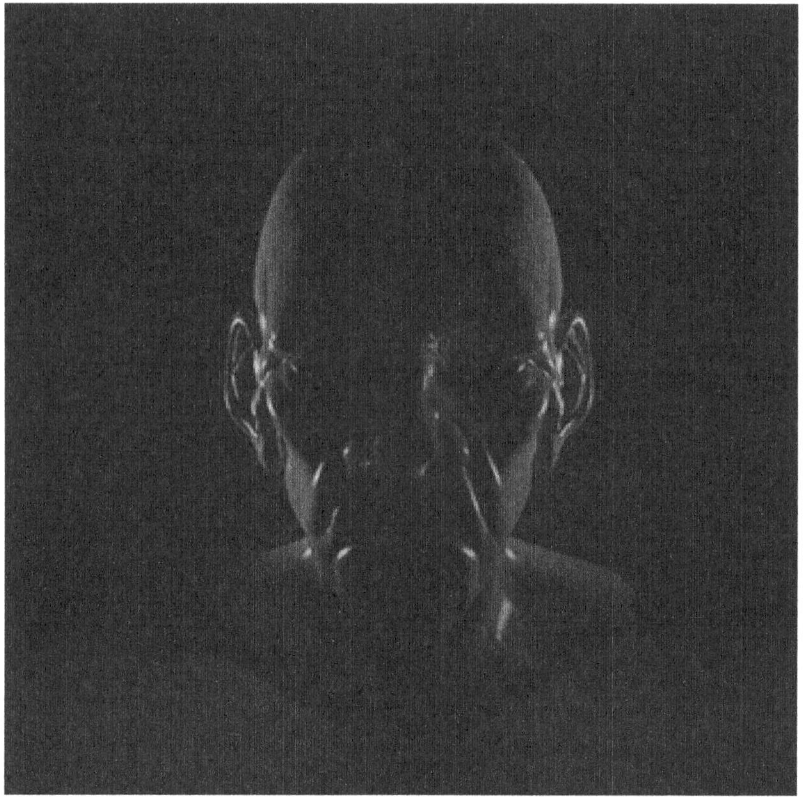

What you see in the previous figure is a typical setup of two lights enhancing the contour of the object. I chose spot lights to give it a sharper look, contrasting with the softness of the rest of the lights. They are placed behind and pointing to the object, each one of different temperature, to get a richer variation in the general mood. These lights will help to define the object even more, and also give a nice variation in the general softness, which is usually something that pleases the viewer.

Now that we have seen the light setup independently for each light, the following figure shows you the final result, when combining all the lights involved:

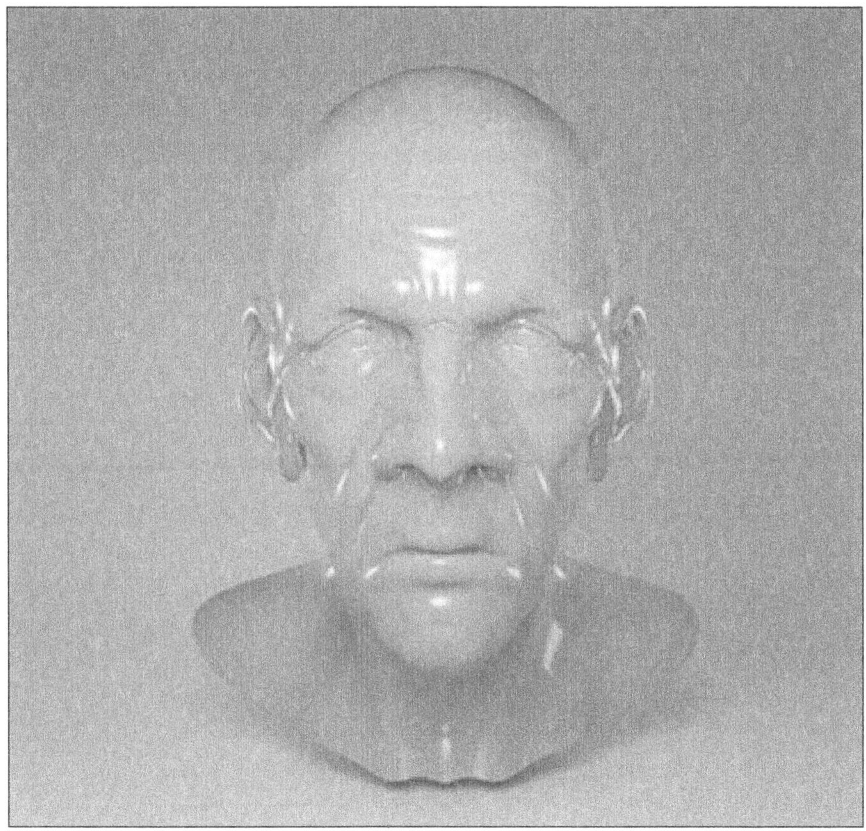

And here you have a classical three point light setup, with its key light, fill light, and contours applied. Notice the richness that the shot shows, well lit frontally, with a nice warm background, subtle but visible, and two different contours, cool and warm, giving it a nice variation in the shading, and a very interesting look.

This applies to situations when you need to light an object, for example, in a typical studio shot.

Summary

At the end of this chapter, you should have learned all the different types of lights you can use as the raw material for lighting.

In the following chapter, we will see deeper how to set up a good illumination in an interior render, where we will apply different kind of lights, and temperatures, and play with the composition.

5
Preparing a Shot

They say the most important thing for a photographer is to know where to stand. The same can be said for the 3D artists when they place the camera. Let's learn some principles and useful tips to get a killer shot (well, figuratively speaking).

The following points will be covered in this chapter:

- Placing the camera
- Depth of Field
- Image sizes

Placing a camera

As with any other element inside of modo, you can place the camera wherever you want. You can also rotate or tilt it by using the handles normally.

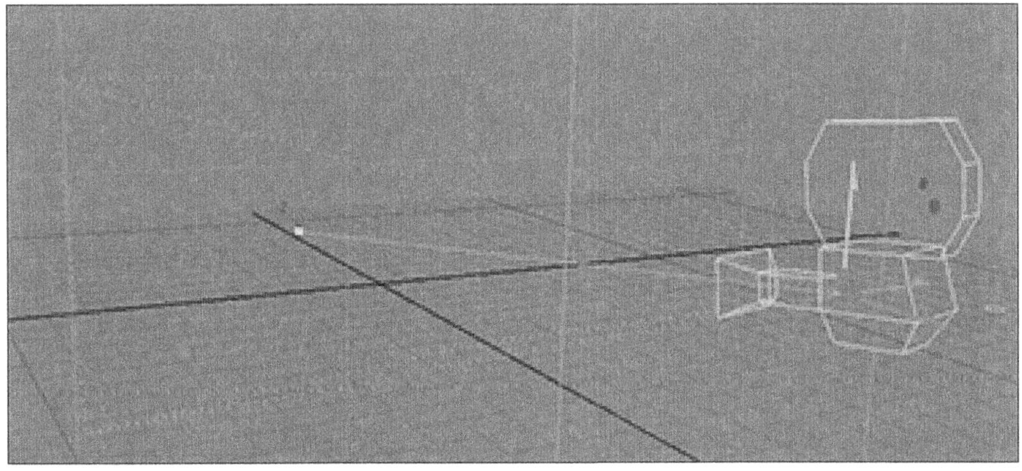

There is also a method for placing the camera more intuitively which lets you see through it as if you were inside it. I recommend you use this second method, as it is the more subjective one.

To look through a camera, choose a viewport and change its View mode to Camera. This will allow you to see through the camera. Once you've changed this setting, you can use the standard keyboard and mouse shortcuts to orient and move the camera.

Remember the following points:

- *Alt* + left-click and drag to rotate
- *Ctrl* + *Alt* + left-click and drag to zoom in and out
- *Shift* + *Alt* + left-click and drag to pan the scene

Knowing the shortcuts will help you to speed up your camera manipulation, but, of course, you can still use the viewport's buttons located in the top-right corner.

Note that, by default, the camera is not visible in the viewport. To fix this, select your camera in the item's list. Then in the **Properties** panel, go to the **Display** tab, and in the **Visible** field, change the value to **YES**. After that, your camera will be visible in the viewport like other objects. This applies for light items too.

Another way of toggling the visibility of the camera and other items or properties on and off is by using the Pie Menu (*Ctrl* + *1*).

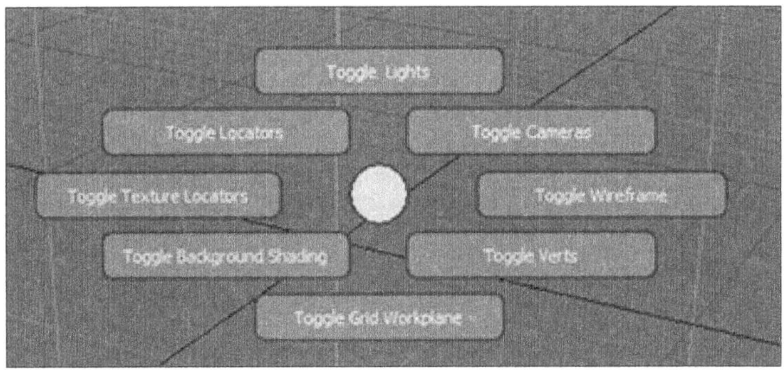

If you hold *Ctrl* + *1*, the Pie Menu will let you choose between different aspects of the elements of the scene you want / do not want to be visible. It's a faster and more practical way than going to every item's properties and will save you a lot of clicks.

This Pie Menu works only in the **Model** tab. If you activate it out of the **Model** tab, you will find different items and options to toggle.

Now that we know how to move the camera, the next question will be *how* to place it. Let's check some tips and tricks to get a nice shot.

Working with the Rule of Thirds

Also known as *The Golden Rule*, the Rule of Thirds helps artists frame compositions that are more pleasing to the eye. It is a method for placing focal points in an image.

This method consists of placing two vertical and horizontal lines dividing the image uniformly. The points where these lines cross are supposed to be more important for the viewer, as the eyes go naturally to those particular points.

Courtesy: www.photographymad.com

This method allows us to set some strong points—in terms of focality—in the image. That is, the point where the attention of the viewer will go in a natural way.

The easiest way of locating a focal point in an image is to place the object we want to catch the attention of the viewers right in the center. This is technically correct, but in terms of composition, it will give us more problems than benefits, because a central focal point means symmetry, and an image with a feeling of symmetry totally loses the extra visual punch that you can get by using the Rule of Thirds. Consider the following screenshot:

It's just a random scene with an object on a background. As I mentioned before, there is an object right in the center, so we make sure that the focal point is there. But, on the other hand, take a look at the general feel of the image. All centered, all straight lines, all homogeneous. The result is a boring picture. Now look at the following one, with slightly different composition:

What about this one? If you imagine the Rule of Thirds overlay, you will notice that I have lowered the horizon line so it matches the bottom guide of the rule, and I have also moved the hippo so its face matches the better focal point.

This can be tricky at first. But once you get used to it, you will be able to use the trick without having to deal with overlays or guidelines. A very simplified approach to this would be the following rule:

Don't put your focal point right in the center. Move it slightly to a corner and try at the same time to leave some empty space in the opposite corner. If you can get a composition that gives the viewer that feeling of empty corner versus full corner, the golden rule is working.

One more quick example: the photographer just made the shot trying to get the horizon line away from the center, matching the top line, and the subject—the dog—again away from the center. But I bet the guy who took this picture just made sure that the dog is not centered and the opposite corner feels "empty". This helped the picture to have a nice sense of composition. I bet you can "feel" the Rule of Thirds in the following image:

Courtesy: mysopoco.wordpress.com

Understanding the field of view

Ever wondered how you can get such an aggressive and cool looking shot as you have seen in many pictures such as the following one? Those kinds of pictures look impressive, dramatic, and full of action. You can get that effect in modo by using the **Field of View** (**FOV** from now on):

Courtesy: http://www.avabeijing.com.cn/english/productxx-102-140-380.html

Controlling the FOV is done through the Angle of View control or through the Focal Length control.

To access the FOV control, select your camera item in the item's list. Then, navigate to **Properties** | **Projection** and you will find a field labeled **Focal Length**, which is **50mm** by default. If you keep lowering that value, you will see—from the camera view—how your scene gets more and more distorted, showing more space in the same image size.

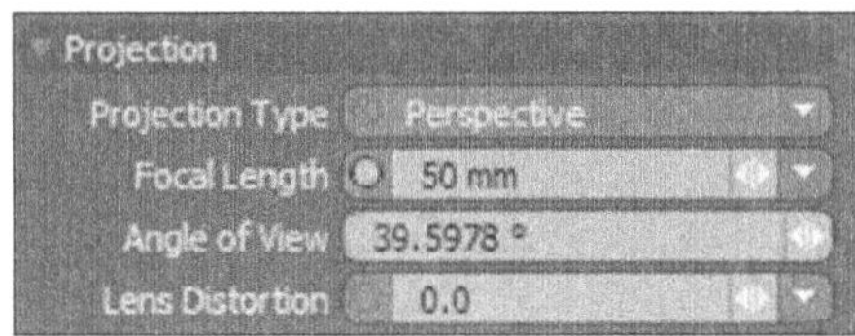

Let me show the differences between a standard 50mm FOV value in a sample scene:

And compare it to the same scene with a FOV value of 20mm:

The difference is clear. The second image shows an extra punch due to the low FOV value. The perspective gets more radical and exaggerated, making it more interesting.

However, you should be careful when lowering the FOV because an excessively low value can give you an unnatural look that you don't want. As always, the effect must be subtle but noticeable.

Tilting the shot

Tilting is another way to put some drama into a shot. This effect is usually tricky to use because it's a more artistic approach to a shot.

It's not a technique generally used for presenting work to clients because the composition can distract from the subject. The approach of this shot is to try to have some kind of dramatic and eye-catching shot that calls for the viewer's eye, but it is better—if you decide to use it—to keep it for things such as portfolio covers, headers, and so on—in general, something that doesn't need to contain specific information about the scene, such as a hook to catch the attention of the other more formal renders.

Courtesy: http://jamphotography.myfotojournal.com/2011/jul/07/randal-jean-family-wrightsville-beach-nc/

Fixing the verticals

As a general rule, a formal way to show a render, especially in architectural works, is to make sure that your verticals are fixed. What does this mean?

When placing the camera to make the shot, you will do it manually, looking for a good spot. You will move the camera up and down, re-orienting it until you get something that convinces you. Due to the fact that your eye and hand aren't perfect tools, there will always be some tilting in the shot, either vertical or horizontal.

If you look at the previous image, I have oriented the camera upwards to make the shot, but if you look at the verticals, they are all tilted and convergent. Although this can be a desired effect to add some "drama" to the scene, it's not the best way to present your image to a client; so we will fix those verticals in a quick, easy way:

Rotation X	0.0 °
Y	106.8974 °
Z	0.0203 °
Order	ZXY

Look for the camera item in the item's list. In its **Properties** panel, you will see the rotation values. The rotation axis that's causing the verticals to tilt is the x axis. So, to remove the effect, just change its value to `0`. You will get the following result:

You can see now that the verticals are totally vertical and straight, no matter which part you are looking at. But there's a side effect to this. If you notice the difference, the shot now shows a bit of offset, as if the camera changed its height. To fix this, we will use the offset control located in the bottom of the **Properties** panel:

This control pans the shot vertically or horizontally without moving the camera, so it's very useful for correcting the natural offset when fixing the verticals. Our shot has moved up, so we will change the Y value in the offset control—just slide the control until you relocate the shot to your liking—until you get the camera height right and the verticals straight; something like the following:

Adding depth using DOF

Depth of Field (also known as **DOF**) is an optical phenomenon related to focus. For a beginner's eyes, a photograph can be in focus or out of focus (when it looks blurred), but in a more advanced way, this is not absolutely true.

It's important to understand that in the real world, a scene will show some parts in focus while others will be out of focus. There will be a certain distance to the camera where things look nice and sharp. We call this point the **focal distance**.

The focal distance is crucial when applying the DOF effect, because this will set the exact point from where things will start to get blurred the more they move away. In other words, the further you get from the focal distance, the more blur you get.

In the following image, you can see two examples of DOF using a different focal distance. The image on the left shows a short focal distance—that's near to the camera—while in the right-hand image, it's moved far away from the camera, showing different focal points:

You can clearly see the effect you can achieve by using DOF. It can dramatically change the focus of the viewer, letting you move the focus of attention to various points in the image.

When to use it

The DOF effect is not always present—at least, not in a noticeable way—so we will have to determine when to use it. By default, DOF is disabled in modo.

In short, we could say the DOF effect is more present in shots of a small scale, things that are little, or shots where the camera is very close to one of the objects even if it's not of a small scale. The closer the camera, the stronger the blurring. The smaller the scene, the more intense the DOF will be. Take a look at the following image:

Courtesy: http://es.m.wikipedia.org/wiki/Archivo:Ballpen_head_macro.jpg

This image would be the best example of DOF working in a small scene. It's just the tip of a ballpoint pen. Notice the intense DOF: the top of the pen is sharp, but that sharpness fades rapidly with distance.

The next image would also be a good example of when to use it. It's not a small scene in any way, but there is an object very close to the camera, making the rest of the scene go out of focus:

Courtesy: http://www.matandwhitney.com/2010_06_01_archive.html

In this case, we are not dealing with a small scale scene in any way. It's a statue attached to a building. But here, we are working with distances. The distance from the camera to the statue is small, and the camera's focus is on the statue. The distance to the background from the camera is much farther than the focal distance, and as such, the DOF on the background is pronounced.

Keeping the example of this image in mind, can help you achieve similar results in modo when creating your own shots using DOF.

When to avoid it

We should avoid DOF in situations when the shot doesn't have a dominant focal point. That is, when there is little difference between distance to camera and distance of visible backgrounds. A large scale scene such as the following is a good example:

Courtesy: http://rapgenius.com/Big-l-deadly-combination-remix-lyrics#note-1613676

If you look at the picture, you will notice there is not a very well defined focal point. Everything is homogeneous and very even, and the attention of the viewer is not guided to any point in particular because there is no DOF visible. In the real world, there is no DOF noticeable in such situations, so if you are working in a large scale scene, my advice is to not use this effect if you don't want to make your shot look like you're looking at a miniature; a DOF effect applied to a scene out of context will make it look like a maquette, which is an interesting effect, but it's not the one we are looking for. We call this effect "tilt shifting".

Courtesy: http://www.taringa.net/posts/imagenes/15467004/Fotografias-con-efecto-Tilt-Shift-geniales.html

The preceding image shows a photo manipulation, giving DOF to a picture that shouldn't have it. That's the "maquette" effect I was talking about. It's not necessary when creating most realistic renders.

How to create it

In order to generate DOF inside of modo, we should work with the camera's properties. Let's see the steps you have to take to generate some DOF in the scene. We will render an image of a chicken with a rhino in the background, putting the focal point on the chicken and leaving the rest out of focus.

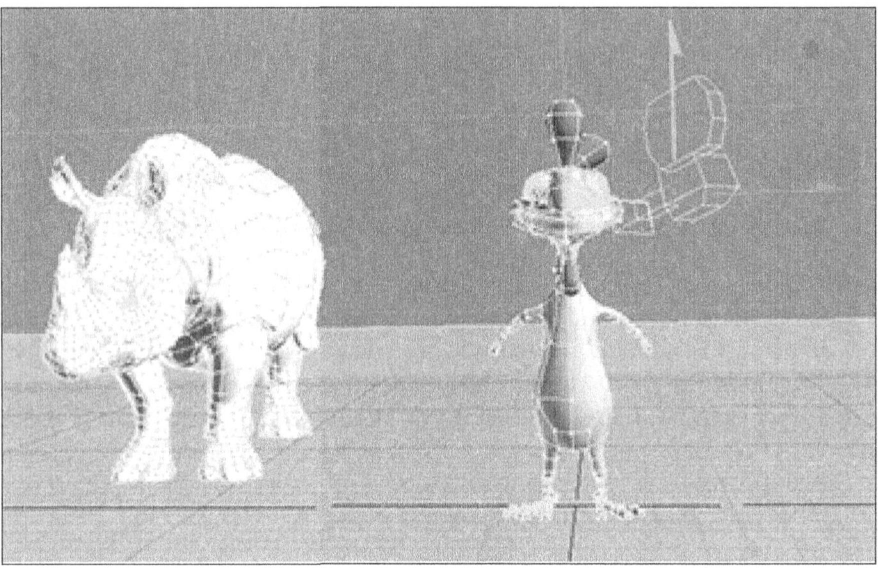

First of all, select your camera in the Items list and look at its **Properties** panel. Inside, you will find a tab labeled **Camera Effects**, and inside of that there will be a section called **Depth of Field**.

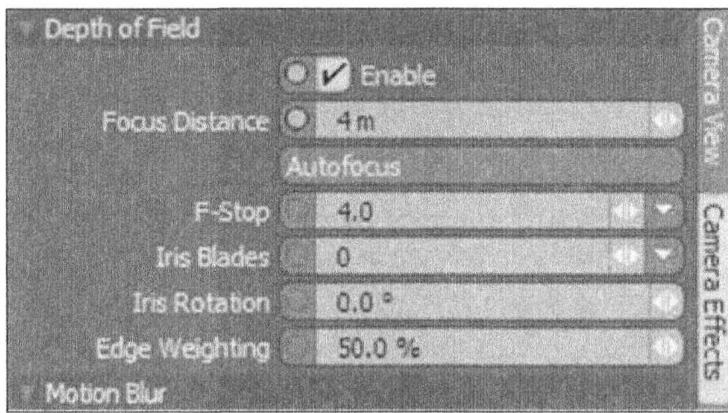

Once in this tab, make sure to check the **Enable** option so the DOF becomes active. You will see many fields in this tab, but again, we will focus on the main options you need to work with to create a good, editable DOF:

- **Focus Distance**: This is the distance (from the camera) where the focal point will be. This point will be in perfect focus, while every other object will become more blurred the further it is from that distance.
- **Autofocus**: If you enable this button, the focal distance will be calculated automatically based on the position of the camera. It can be useful for certain scenes, such as wide angles and panoramic shots, but can become tricky to work with when in very close shots. Choose whether you want it or not based on the kind of scene you are working on.
- **F-Stop**: This controls the intensity of the blur. The lower the number, the stronger the blur.

You can also control the DOF visually by looking at the camera item representation in the viewport. You should see a dotted pyramid shape coming out of the camera's lens.

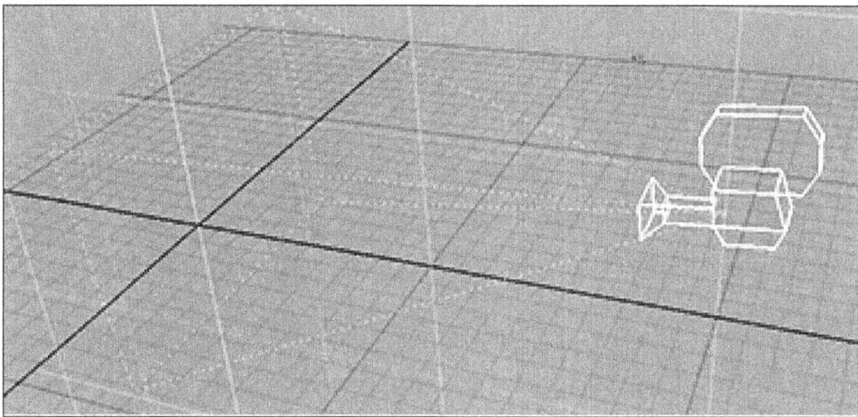

That pyramid is in fact a visual representation of the focal distance and is only visible when the **Camera** item is selected. You can try to adjust the focal distance in the camera's **Properties** panel and notice how the **Camera** item in the viewport changes the length of the pyramid to express the focal distance. This is helpful to know where exactly is this point located without having to experiment in a hit-and-miss procedure.

Once you set the focal distance, it's a good practice to set the **F-Stop** value to establish how strong you want the blur of the out-of-focus areas:

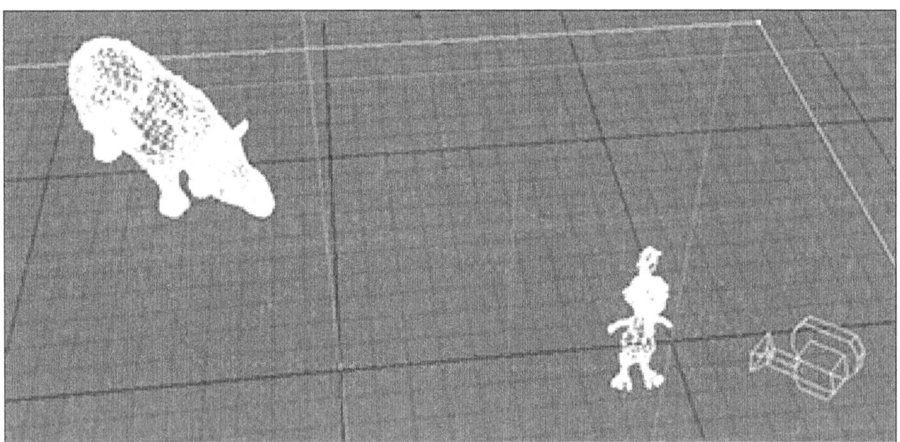

Notice how the pyramid touches the rhino establishing that it will be the focal distance. So the rhino will be in focus while the chicken will not. I also lowered the **F-Stop** value from the default `4.0` to `2.0`, so the blur will be stronger. The following is the result:

Choosing the correct image size

In terms of output, the render size is an important matter because it will extremely affect the render times—larger images require more render time—and depending on the final output, you will need to adjust sizes and depth (dots per inch) of the image. Let's see the main concerns you will have when deciding on your image size.

Size and image depth (dpi)

When talking about image size, everyone knows what we are talking about, right? We are talking about how many pixels there are in length and in width. First of all, we must know how to set up your scene with a certain image size and this is controlled by the **Render** properties, in the **Shader Tree**:

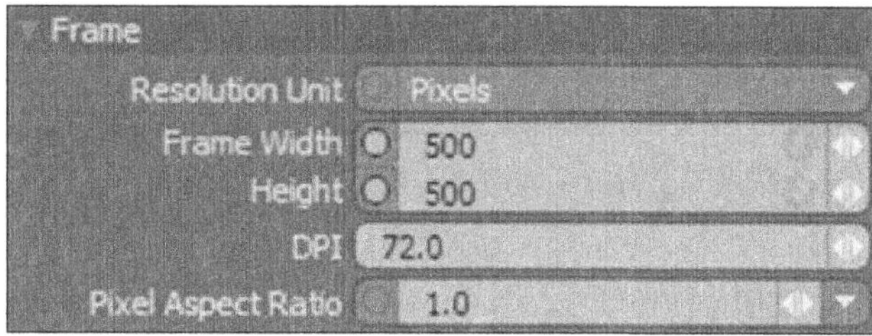

In the section named **Frame**, you will find many fields to tweak the size of the rendered image. Let's focus on what's important:

- **Resolution Unit**: This is a matter of taste. You can choose the units you want for your size from this drop-down menu. The options are **Pixels**, **Inches**, and **Centimeters**. If you are from the USA, maybe you would prefer to use inches. If you are more into graphic design, using pixels as your unit could be the best idea. It's not important really, just use the one that fits your needs better.
- **Frame Width / Frame Height**: Self-explanatory. Just put the values you want for your image size.
- **DPI**: This is the value of dots per inch for the output. It expresses the density of the image. We will discuss it more in depth in the next section.

Rendering for printing

The first thing I ask my clients when collecting information for a project is: "Will you print it?"

This might sound trivial, but in fact this is a crucial question for you as the producer of the image. There is a huge difference in size when talking about print sizes or screen sizes. The main concern is that print sizes are way bigger than screen sizes, so it will greatly affect your render times when having to deal with big render sizes.

Along with image size, the difference comes from the **dots per inch** (**DPI**) value of the image. So, what is that DPI thing?

The quality of a printing (apart from image size) is heavily related to its DPI. This expresses the number of pixels present in a squared inch. The more the number of pixels, the more dense the image and the better the quality. Take a look at a comparison of low and high DPI images:

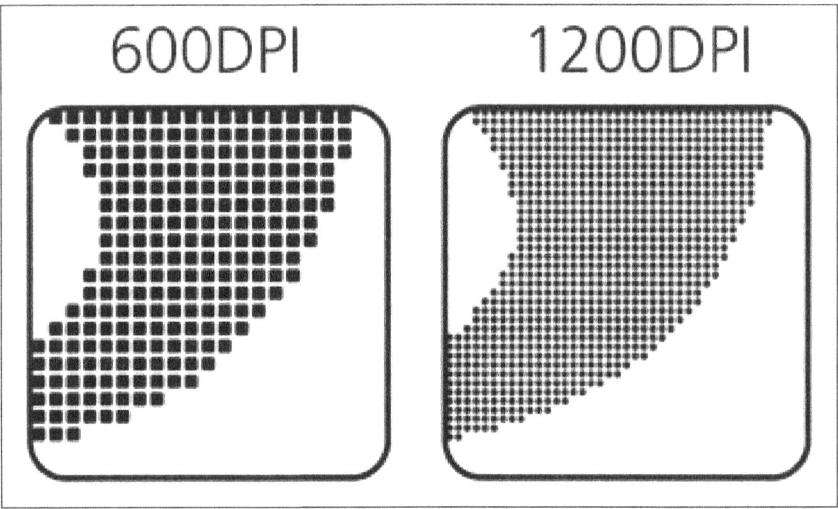

Courtesy: http://www.inktechnologies.com/blog/understanding-printer-resolution/

DPI only has meaning when it comes to printing images. On a computer monitor, this is irrelevant because there are only pixels. The more the number of pixels, the better the quality. But printing an image, in the sense of representing an image on a physical media, needs to have the DPI setting present to get a good quality.

As a common rule, always have in mind that DPI is only relevant when dealing with rendering frames in inches or centimeters, not in pixels.

So, how many DPI should I set up for my print? It depends on the size of it. The larger the print, the more DPI you'll want to get. My advice is to use 300 DPI as a basis and increase the value as you increase the image size. If you want to print an A4 size image, I would use a regular DPI of 300. If you want a larger size, such as an A3 or A2 size, don't be afraid to double it to 600, or even 1200 if you are asked to print a big poster.

Of course, there is an image size (in pixels) assigned to each paper size. We could use the following chart to know the size/DPI we will want for our printings (in rounded up numbers):

- **A4 (regular magazine size)**: 3500 x 2500 / 300 DPI
- **A3**: 5000 x 3500 / 450 DPI
- **A2**: 7000 x 5000 / 600 DPI
- **A0 (poster)**: 15000 x 10000 / 1200 DPI

Rendering for digital media

If your client only wants to show the rendered image on his/her laptop or tablet, or even on a big TV screen, you are only concerned about pixels, because DPI is irrelevant for these kinds of outputs.

Nowadays, for a modern workstation, it is common to render a full HD image (1920 x 1080) on a day-to-day basis. A good rule is to always ask your client what resolution they need from you or to find out what final output they're targeting.

Maybe he/she will want to show it on a full HD TV set, maybe on a tablet, maybe on a laptop. Your first thought would be to make the render size exactly the same as the screen size you will be using. That's correct, but there is a better method.

When working with digital media outputs, you will find a standard size of 1920 x 1080 pixels. In future, the image size of a monitor will be higher for sure, but for now, we will take this as a standard of high quality. If you want to get the most from your render, don't stick to the screen size; at least double it. In the graphic design world, when talking about 3D renders for digital media, it's very common to have sizes of 4000 pixels for a raw render.

So, regardless of the screen size your client wants to use, go ahead and launch a good 4000-pixel wide render, then scale it down to the final output size and you will see a nice benefit in quality along with some other beneficial side effects such as noise removal or crisper lines. If you are short on time or don't have the system required to finish such a big render, stick to the final size.

So, to have an overall view of image sizes/DPI according to the output, we will follow the following simple rules:

- **For printings**: Render at least at 300 DPI. Raise it as the paper size increases.
- **For digital media**: Make a big 4000-pixel wide render and scale it down to the final size.

Summary

You have learned the basic steps and procedures to place your camera with some sense of how to get a decent shot. You have also learned how to express certain things and how to call to attention a specific point of an image, finding the right composition and deciding the output depending on the medium on which your image will be displayed.

We can now move on to the next chapter where we will dive into the very core of 3D—the fine art of making a good render. The main points covered will be setting up the render to optimize the image the best we can and understanding the basic concepts of Global Illumination so we can mimic a natural and visually appealing illumination.

6
Rendering your Scene

This chapter will be one of the most important parts of Luxology modo learning since rendering and knowing how to get a good image is the ultimate goal of any 3D artist.

Let's learn how to achieve this by studying the following topics:

- Understanding indirect illumination
- MonteCarlo vs irradiance caching
- HDRI illumination
- Using the physical sky simulation
- Setting up the render
- Rendering with the preview window
- Working with the render window

Understanding indirect illumination

Indirect illumination is the method used by 3D software to mimic the behavior of light in the real world, mostly referring to the light bounce effect, enabled by default in modo701.

Courtesy by http://s3.media.squarespace.com/production/1163872/15347329/wp-content/uploads/2011/03/LightBounce_thumb.jpg

I have provided a sample figure to demonstrate the light bounce effect in the real world. The image is over-saturated, so the effect gets very noticeable. We have an orange in a white environment, lit by the sunlight. There are lit areas and shadowy areas, but take a look at the zone where the ground meets the orange. You will notice an orange tinting in the ground (the same color as the fruit). That is the light coming from the sun, bouncing off the orange skin and hitting the floor, coloring it with the tone captured from the bounce.

That's the effect we will achieve when using indirect illumination, and that's the way to create a radically different look in your image. Let's check it step by step:

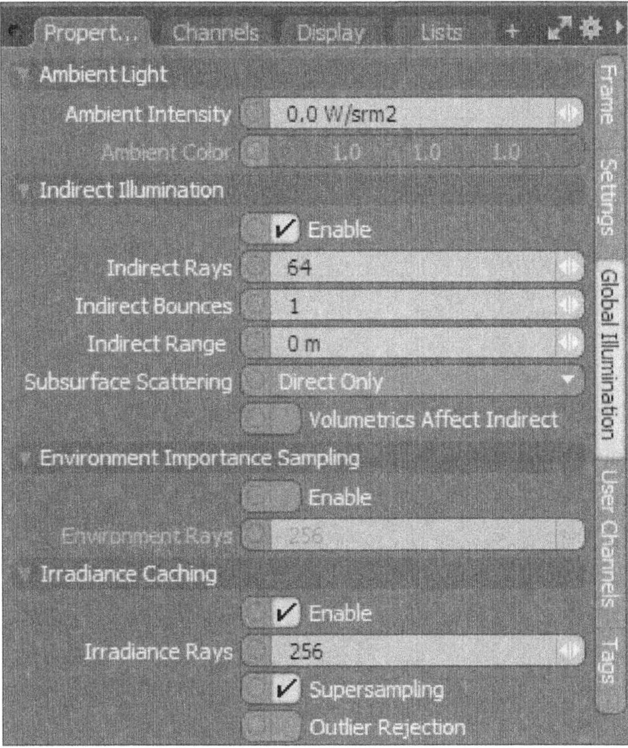

To locate the controls for indirect illumination, you must go to your **Shader Tree** and under the **Shading** tab, click on the **Render** item, then in its **Properties** panel go to the **Global Illumination** tab. There, you will find the settings related to **Indirect Illumination**, containing the following fields:

- **Ambient Intensity**: This field is disabled by default. It controls the overall luminosity in the scene. It can be useful in getting some extra brightness in a hard-to-light scene by raising the value slightly. The more you raise it, the brighter the scene becomes, but it tends to flatten the image. So, my advice would be not to use it unless it's totally necessary.

- **Indirect Rays**: This field lets you set the number of rays involved in the bouncing calculation. More the number of rays, more precise will be the shading of the scene, but at the cost of more render time, of course. A smaller number will generate blotchiness or poorly shaded areas and graininess. Too high a number and the render time will become too long. You need to find the right balance.

As a general rule, exterior shots lit by the sunlight, need way less rays to get a good result, while interior shots or scenes with areas hard to reach by light, will need more rays.

The previous image shows the same scene with a lower number of rays (left) versus a higher number of rays (right). You can notice the graininess caused by a lower rays setting. In the right image, the render shows fine but the render time and rays number need to be extremely high, making it unviable for real work. Consider it as an example.

- **Indirect Bounces**: This field sets the number of bounces for the light. There is a practical range to establish this number. The lower range of number to get color tinting and nicely shaded areas is something in between 2-3. If you want finer shading, more intense color tinting, and better distribution of light, you can raise it up to something like 5. Theoretically, it is said that light in the real world cannot bounce more than 16 times (that's 16 bounces) because it looses a big chunk of energy with each bounce. So, after the 16th bounce, the ray doesn't have but a tiny bit of energy left, thus there will be no noticeable effects. As per my experience, the general rule would be five bounces for interior scenes and two for exteriors.

The previous image shows the difference between one bounce and eight bounces. It is clear that the 8-bounces image (obviously the right one) shows way better shading, finer color tinting, and a more even distribution of light, getting a more natural look at the expense of more render time, than the 1-bounce image.

- **Indirect Range**: This is a kind of trick that you will find really helpful with hard-to-light scenes, when there is a lack of time to complete the render, or just while making a quick preview of the scene.

What the **Indirect Range** method does is limit the distance the rays will travel, thus saving rendering time and calculations required, but on the other hand, the result will not be as accurate or realistic as it would have been with a full calculation. Let's take a look at the following scene:

The previous figure is a test scene from `www.3dallusions.com`, perfect to show the **Indirect Range** method. There are two images: the top image shows a high range while the bottom shows a low range. The difference is very noticeable in the bottom image, where the shading only spreads over a short distance, leaving the rest unshaded. These are two extreme examples, so we must find a balance in order to get a good shading distance. I would set up the scene in the following manner:

As you see, I applied a mid-way distance between too high and too low visually. The point of the setting is to find a value that covers mostly everything in the scene, so you cannot see unshaded areas, but at the same time not raising it too much, so that you avoid an excessive dark look.

There are pros and cons for this method. As I said earlier, it's good to render a quick image since the shading distance is fixed, but the overall look will become less natural and accurate than a full calculation (leaving **Indirect Range** as zero). The other benefit is in the fact that you don't need to put lights to get lighting. If you just set an environment color (preferably white to get a neutral coloring), the distance method will assure that every single corner will receive light and shading (if the distance allows it).

In short, if you want a quick render (but with an acceptable quality), use the **Indirect Range** method. It proves good for quick productions, or to cut down render time in animations, where you need to render hundreds of images.

- **Irradiance Caching**: This field is enabled by default. It is an interpolated method for calculating the extent of shading. If you enable it, you will get faster renders, but they will be lesser accurate. We will see the differences in depth in the next section.

Montecarlo versus irradiance caching

Basically, there are two methods for calculating the final image in the render. Montecarlo is an algorithm that calculates the trajectory of the rays casted to get the correct shading. This method is tedious and filled with calculations, but totally accurate. The irradiance caching method is interpolated, so you get faster calculations, but they are lesser accurate.

Using the montecarlo method

The **montecarlo** (**MC**) method involves a complete calculation, with no interpolation at all. It works on a brute force calculation.

Let's get back to the box scene but with a light in the ceiling. The polygon acting as a light is just a material with the **Luminous Intensity** field enabled (see *Chapter 3, Texturing and Materials* for reference). To illustrate the MC method, we will disable **Irradiance Caching** and see what happens:

The MC method assigns a number of rays to the light source and then casts them from the light to the scene, just like in the real world. This is why we see all the graininess in the scene. The number of rays is too low, so the scene will not be totally covered by rays. The fix for that would be raising the number of rays. Let's raise it:

Now that's better. There are more rays, so the surfaces get more density when covered by them. But it's still not enough to get rid of the noise, or graininess as we call it. If you want to get a noise-free image with this method, you will need to really crank up the amount of rays, sometimes to crazy values. The following image is noise free with MC:

Here, you can see the true power of MC: totally accurate and physically correct shading, but with crazy render times. If you have the time to let it cook overnight, just go ahead and you will get magnificent shading and illumination. Depending on the scene, expect render times above 10 hours in case of heavy scenes.

The irradiance caching method

The **irradiance caching** (IC) method is a more productive way to set up your render. This method is based on a two-passes procedure. The first pass will be casting a number of rays to statistically determine the shading of every area of the scene. Then, it makes a second pass calculating the interpolated values that will confirm the final image.

This is the true power of IC: it's fast.

Please have a look at the previous figure. In the left image, you can see the pre-pass stage that determines the base to calculate the final shading. In the right-hand side image, the final render is completed based on the previous calculation. This is a pretty simple scene, so you can virtually see no differences with a noise free MC render in just a fraction of time.

Using HDRI illumination

HDRI stands for high dynamic range image. It's an image format, just like JPEG, but with more information in it. While JPEG contains information about color (RGB values), the HDRI format contains information about luminosity, which makes it a good tool to be used as a light source.

Courtesy: www.web3dnews.org

Right inside modo's library, you can see a lot of HDRI images (in the `Environment` folder). Just select one and drag it into your scene. You can use whichever image you want (as long as it is in the HDRI format). There are a lot of sites across the Internet where you can find good quality HDRI images. I recommend you to take a look at `http://hdrmaps.com/freebies`.

Normally, we will use a plain color or maybe a range of colors from the **Environment Material** item to generate a general shading. By using HDRI images, we will get way better and richer shading and toning in our images, especially in exterior shots. For this very reason, a VFX supervisor will take a panoramic HDRI so that any **Computer Generated Image** (**CGI**) to be added to a scene will have the correct environment lighting.

Let me show you a quick scene lit by just an environment color:

I just created a porcelain material, and left the **Environment Material** value by default. Now, I will throw an HDRI right into the scene. See the difference:

As you can see, just by opening the **Preset** panel, selecting the **Environment** folder, and dragging the one of your choice right into the viewport, it will be automatically assigned to the environment, casting its own light to the scene. We get great reflections, great shading, and a way richer scene overall, just by using this technique.

To me, there is no real limitation on using this. Just use it whenever you want to and don't stick to plain colors with your environments. This will give an extra punch to your images. It also ensures better integration between CG and live action footage or images. It sells the CG as *real*.

Using the physical sky simulation

Inside modo, we can use the built-in physical sky environment. It is obviously used to mimic real world conditions concerning the sun position, color of the sky, and so on.

By using this, we don't need to eyeball a real daylight scene. Instead, we just need to enable the physically-based daylight and tweak its parameters until we are happy with the results.

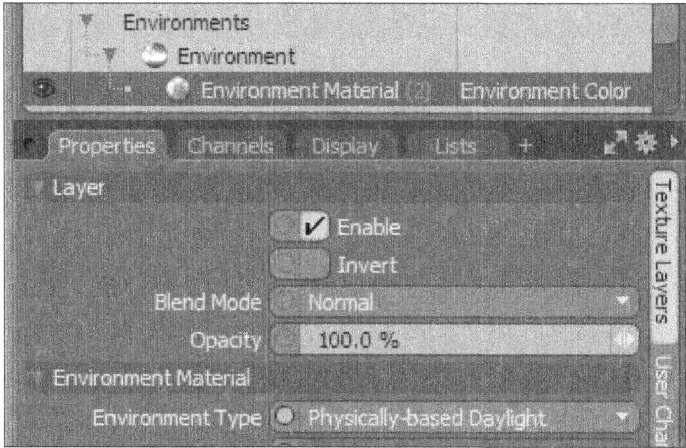

To enable it, go to the **Environment** item under your shader tree and click on it to expand. At the end of the group, you will see the **Environment Material** option. Click on it to select and go to its properties. In its **Properties** panel, you will see a drop-down clickable menu labeled **Environment Type**. From the given options, choose **Physically-based Daylight**. Now, it's done. We have our real sky working.

Adding sunlight

Once the daylight system is enabled, it will only change the color and luminosity of the sky. We need to add a real sun. You can leave it as it is and control the sun with a standard light (directional light is the one with a closer look at the sun), but if you want a fully automatic daylight system, we must enable the physical sun.

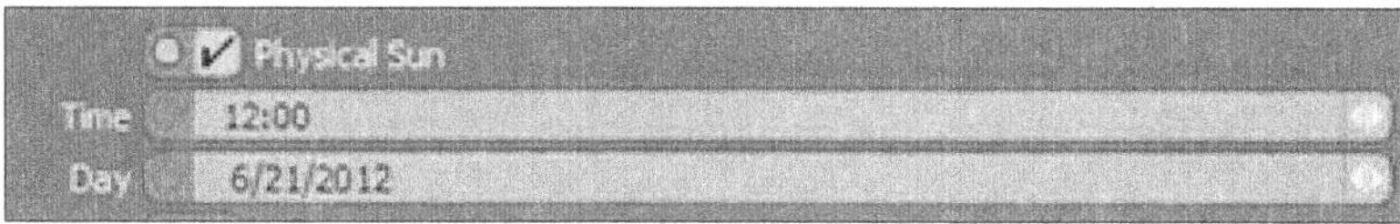

Go to your shader tree again, find the shader panel light item, and expand it. You will see an item called **Directional Light** at its bottom. Select it and go to its **Properties** panel. In this panel, you will see a number of areas. Locate the one called **Physical Sun** (at the bottom of the panel). Once in that section, just enable the **Physical Sun** checkbox.

That pretty much sums up everything. Once you have your sky and sun enabled, you only need to control the time slider to set up the system in a certain hour of the day. The color, luminosity, and sun direction will change automatically according to the hour value. Here, I have dropped a couple of images produced just by using different values for the hour:

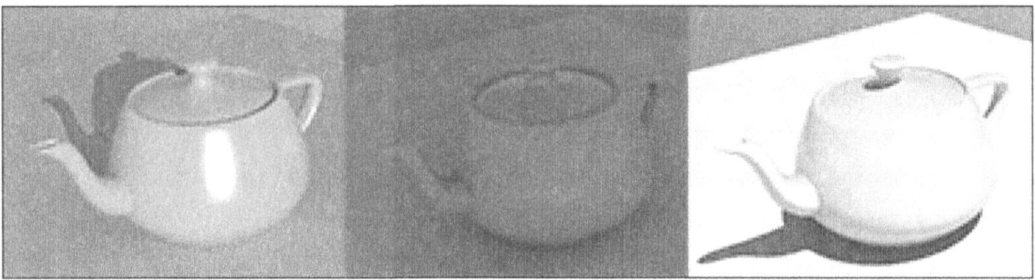

Setting up the render

Now that we know the different aspects of rendering, types of illumination, and so on, it's time for us to deal with the different values that will affect the quality of the image produced.

There is a vast variety of settings inside modo concerning render, but as usual, we will focus only on the main and most important of them. Let's first check the parameters that we must keep in mind to get the most out of our scene. I will provide the complete path to every option under each of the elements.

Indirect rays

Shader Tree | Render | Properties | Global Illumination | Indirect Illumination

When working with the MC method, this value will define the quality of the shading (only if we work with the IC field disabled). As I said earlier, this is a brute force method with nothing interpolated, so the greater the number of rays, higher will be the quality, and longer will the render time be.

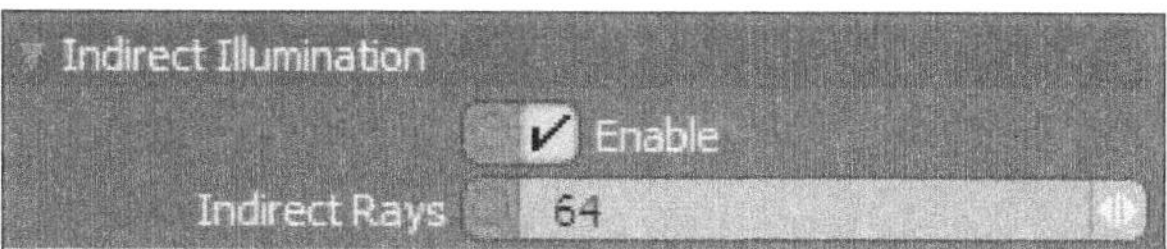

Irradiance rays

Shader Tree | Render | Properties | Global Illumination | Irradiance Caching

This parameter is basically the same as indirect rays, but only when we work with the IC field enabled. This value will set the definition of the shading. The greater the number of rays, the higher the quality of shading will be, along with longer render times. Typically, I would recommend to set it to a value of 2000 for interior shots and 1000 or less for exteriors.

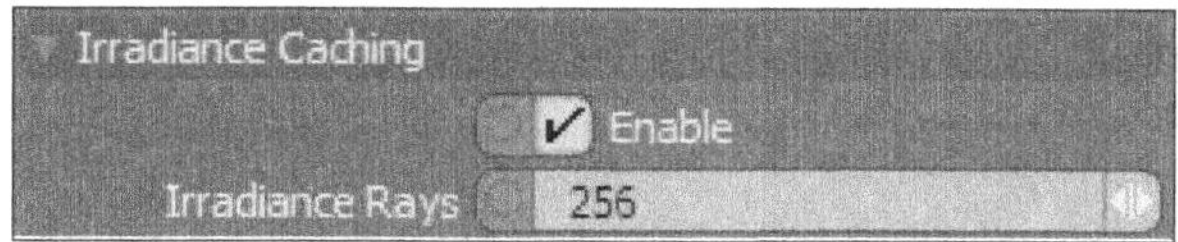

Antialiasing

Shader Tree | Render | Properties | Settings | Antialiasing

This is a filter to fix pixelated borders visible in objects, caused by the size of the image (remember that we are working with a monitor screen, which is basically a grid of pixels). In order to represent diagonal or curvy lines, there will be some pixelation present (or aliasing as we call it). In the next figure, I will show an image that compares the two, without antialiasing and with it enabled, so that you can note the marked difference.

This filter blends the pixelated areas with its boundaries, so visually you will see it as a smooth line. Depending on the scene, you will need higher or lower intensity in the filter. This is controlled by the amount of samples in the **Antialiasing** setting (8 by default). Raise it or lower it until you see no aliasing in your scene.

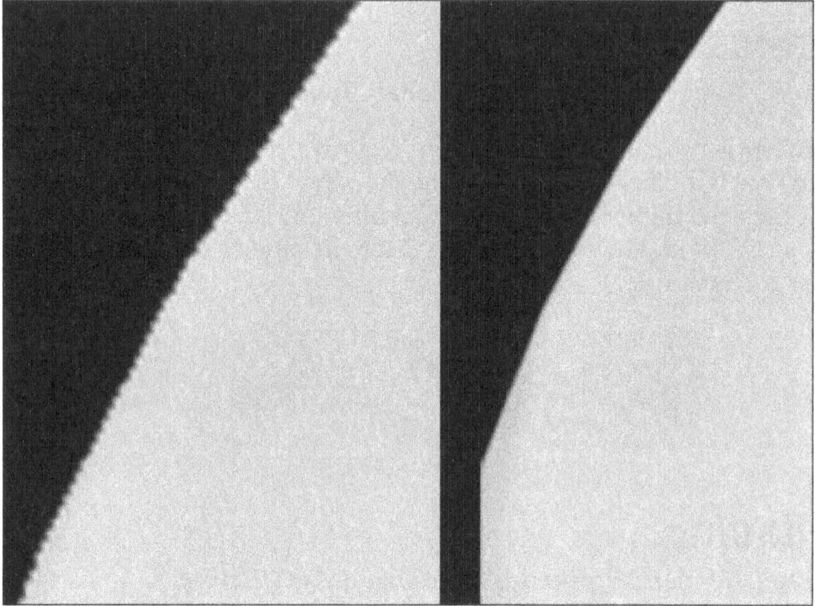

In the previous figure, you can see the images of two zoomed parts of the same scene with different values in the **Antialiasing** filter. The left image is rendered at a minimum antialias (1 Sample/Pixel) while the right one shows a maximum value (1024 Samples/Pixel). The differences are obvious. As usual, find the correct antialiasing value for your scene to get rid of any visible aliasing, and of course, more samples means longer render time.

Rendering with the preview window

In modo, we have two main methods available for rendering our scene. One is the built-in render engine as found in any other 3D software. The other is less used, and that's the one we will talk about in this section. Let me show you how to use the render preview window for a final render.

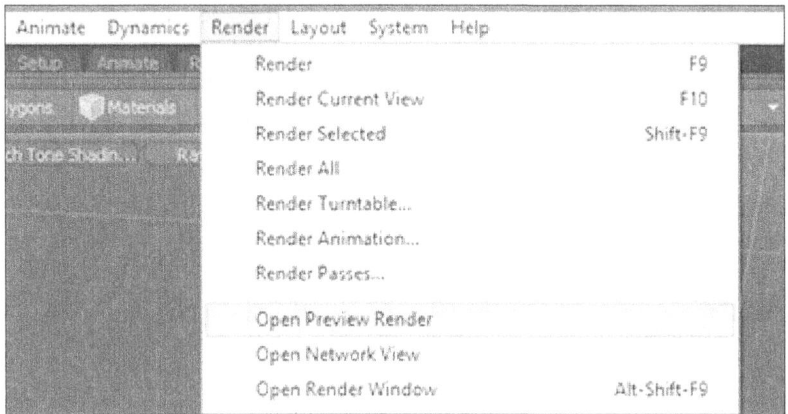

As you should hopefully know by now, you can render your scene by pressing *F9* on your keyboard (or in the top menu by **Render** | **Render**). But if you press *F8* (or **Render** | **Open Preview Render** in the top menu), the preview render window will pop up to show you a real-time, low quality render of the scene. Let's see what it offers:

In this figure, I have built a simple scene with various materials. After setting the environment to be an HDRI and pressing *F8*, the **Preview** window shows what you see. By default, the **Preview** window will show a low quality version of your scene acting as a draft and you can have a good idea of what the image will look like. But there are some options you can tweak so that you can use the preview as a final rendered image.

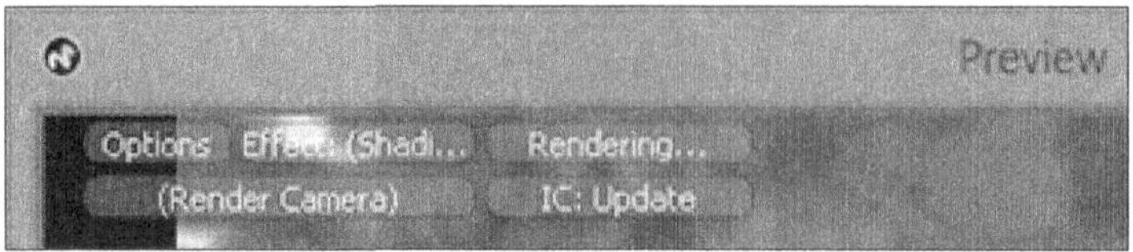

In the top-left corner of the **Preview** window, you will see a bunch of buttons. The one we look for is the one labeled **Options**. Click on it and you will get access to the main options that we can use to turn the preview into a final render. The options we need to tweak are the following:

- **Use All Threads**: This is the option we need to enable to speed up the rendering to our machine's potential. By default, modo doesn't assign all the resources to the preview window because it's mainly designed to provide a quick responsive preview, so must stay light and fast. If you enable the **Use All Threads** options, all the resources will go to the previewer, unleashing its power the way we need it.
- **Full Resolution**: This option must be enabled too. When disabled, the preview window can be resized manually just like any regular window. The render size will then be equal to the window size, so you are, in fact, changing the render size by resizing the window. When enabled, you still can resize the window, but not affect the render size any more. Instead, a percentage number will appear at the bottom-right corner, indicating the relative size of the final image.
- **Quality**: By default, this option is set to **Draft**. There are three modes for **Quality** (**Draft**, **Final**, and **Extended**). I recommend you to set it to **Extended** in order to make your life easier.

When in the **Draft** mode, the quality will be, well in draft. It will just be a quick preview, with low quality shading, and a poor overall look (that's why it's called draft). Don't use it for a final render for obvious reasons.

In the **Final** mode, the rendering will go on refining until it reaches the quality level set in your scene.

The **Extended** mode is the most interesting for us. It continues refining over time, in fact, over passing the quality set in the scene. This is the option we certainly want to use. Enable it.

So, having set the **Preview** window, just let it cook. The image will be refining continuously until it reaches the quality level you want. Being in the **Extended** quality mode, the refining will never stop on itself because it will be polishing the image ad infinitum. Just let it do its work, go for a walk, come back, and see how it looks. The more time you give it, the better result will you get.

If you have enough time, this method is suitable for scenes with the MC sampling method. Making a progressive render (with the preview render) is, in fact, faster (in my experience) than starting a regular render when using MC. Put it in the **Extended** quality mode and let it sample everything.

Besides that, a good trick is using the mouse to refine selective areas. If you have your scene with a pretty decent look and an acceptable level of noise, you may want to clear up some corners or areas harder to sample by the previewer alone. In modo, we can hover the mouse over that area: don't click on anything, just place the pointer there and all the resources will be assigned to the zone where the mouse is hovering.

Working with the render window

If, instead of using a progressive render with the previewer, you want a direct render, you can use the regular render window, accessible by pressing *F9* on your keyboard or navigating to **Render** | **Render** in the top menu.

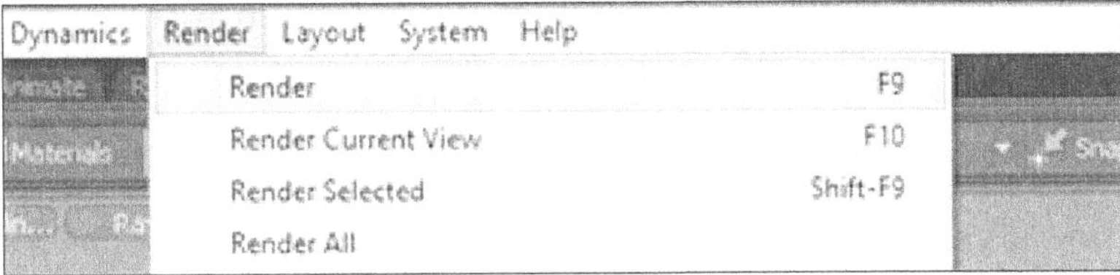

The render window is a more complete tool for rendering due to its internal methods of post-processing and statistics. The following screenshot gives a general overview of what this window looks like:

Basically, the render window is divided into many sections. First is the Final Image panel, where you can see the process of rendering, and where the final image will be displayed for you to save. The right part is full of information about the image and is divided into three tabs.

The first tab is **Image Processing**. Under this area, there will be many options available to process the image once it is completed. There are a lot of advanced options too, but we will focus only on the following discussed ones.

Input white level and tone mapping

Under the **Image Processing** tab, you will find these two fields. The **Input White Level** field controls the overall exposure of the image. Note that this value does not act like a brightness control option but like a real camera exposure, such as the camera iris.

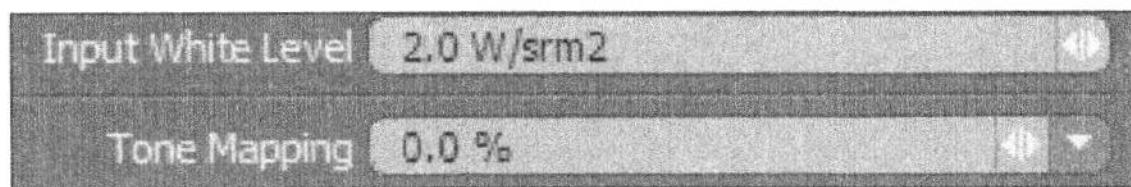

We can play with the possibility of controlling the exposure of the image since the raw render in modo generates an HDRI image, which contains light information. Play with it to change the exposure of the image. This control is inversely proportional, so lower values will mean more exposure and vice versa. Take a look at how this value affects the figure:

That's the image rendered. After the rendering process is complete, I've played with the **Input White Level** values. From left to right, the values are `10.0`, `2.0`, and `0.5` W/srm2. You can see that as the value lowers down, the image gets more exposure.

The **Tone Mapping** control works like a post-processing effect that controls how the excess amount of light gets redistributed. Typically, what I do is set the exposure value until I get the exposure I want and then fine tune it with the **Tone Mapping** tool.

Take a look at the most exposed image. The clarity of the image can be correct, but it's all blown up by light. If you go to the **Tone Mapping** value and raise it, the excess amount of light will get redistributed and you will get rid of the problematic areas. Look at the following figure:

The left image shows the render at a low **Input White Level** value (`0.5` in this case). As you can see, it's completely blown out. But if you want to preserve that exposure, you can raise the **Tone Mapping** value to fix the overexposure. This is an extreme case, so you can see the effect clearly. The **Tone Mapping** control is directly proportional, that is higher the number, more intense will be the light correction. In this particular image, the exposure (the **Input White Level** value) was set to `0.5` and the **Tone Mapping** value was at `100%`.

Bloom and vignette

These two values are more of an extra addition to the image than as image fixing tools like the input white level and tone mapping tools.

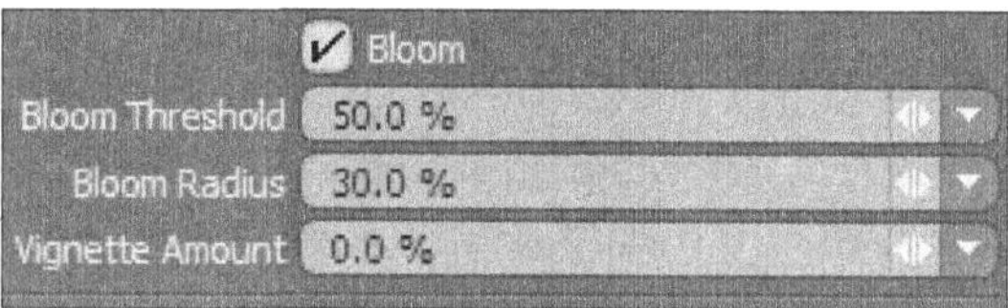

The **Bloom** effect is a lighting effect that creates a glimmery look in those areas where the light is more intense. If the scene is homogeneous in terms of light, it will apply over the entire scene giving a dreamy-like mood, but the main goal of the **Bloom** tool is to mimic the light effect of emitters of overexposed areas in the real world. I will set the same scene with the teapot as an emitter (remember giving its material a luminous intensity value) and see the result:

Now, the teapot is an emitter and is contributing to the lighting of the scene. If you take a look at the **Bloom** control, you will see two values to tweak:

- **Bloom Threshold**: This value controls the amount of light necessary to apply the bloom. The lower the number, the bigger the area that receives the effect.
- **Bloom Radius**: This value controls how far the effect expands from the source of light. The higher the number, more diffused will be the effect.

After playing a bit with the controls for this particular figure, I have come to this:

You can tweak the values until you get the desired effect. This is a good effect to apply in your scenes in order to give it an extra touch of realism, although you'll have to be subtle when applying it to get a convincing look. Take note that I have made an excessive effect, so that you see it clearly.

The second effect you have available here is the **Vignette Amount** control. It is a real effect found in camera lenses, present mostly in shots with low light conditions, where the results are darkened corners. It's pretty simple to use by using the value in the **Vignette Amount** field. Increase the value to get more or decrease it to reduce the effect.

In order to use this effect properly, try to use it only in low light conditions while being present in the real world, and avoid using it in shots like sunny exteriors. The following figure is the same scene with some vignetting applied for you to see how the corners darken:

Render region

Under the **Compare** | **Region** | **Options** tab, you will see the tool we need the most at this level, as it is very useful, called **Render Region**.

When fine tuning a scene, there will be times when you need to focus on a specific area of the image. Let's say you are trying to find the right render adjustments for a specific scene. Everything looks fine, except for some reflections on the floor that look grainy. It will be very unproductive having to render the entire image just to fix one particular area. That is when the **Render Region** tool comes handy. I will give a quick example. Take a look at the following figure:

This is a typical example where you need to use the **Render Region** tool. The scene looks fine, except for the floor's reflection that looks too grainy. Having said that, we will not have to re-render the entire scene just to fix that particular issue only. Here, the **Render Region** tool will come in handy.

In the top menu, go to **Render** | **Render Region** tool. Once activated, draw a rectangle in the visor, defining the area you want to render. In this case, we will draw a rectangle in the reflection area. Now that the region to render has been established, you only need to tweak the render the way you need to fix the problem with the reflection (in this case, I raised the value for rays reflection in the material properties) and then press *F9*. In the render window, you will see how only the defined region is rendered, thus saving time and work.

With the problem fixed, you can now disable the **Render Region** tool. Go to your Shader Tree, then in its **Properties** panel click on the **Frame** tab, and look for the section at the bottom of the panel labeled **Render Region**. Disable it by unticking the checkbox provided beside it.

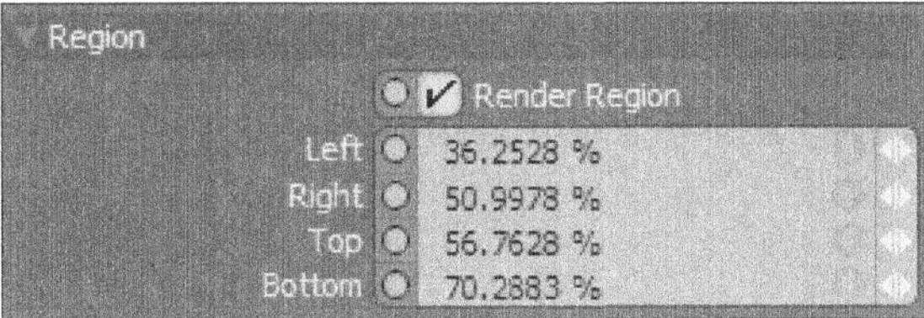

Now, with the **Render Region** option disabled and the issue fixed, you can again press *F9* again to get the final image. The result in this case will be as shown in the following figure:

Once the final image gets completed, go to the bottom of the render window, and click on the **Save Image** button. It's done. You have just produced and saved your first render!

Summary

By the end of this chapter, you do know how to set up a good render, control the lights, and optimize your scene to get the best possible image in the least amount of time.

The process of producing a good image doesn't stop here. We are now moving to the final step which is post-production, where we will enhance the raw render to get a nice final art by using some Photoshop tricks.

7

The Post-production Phase

The final stage of the work is not producing the rendered image. The key to standing out over amateur 3D artists is to control the post-production phase, which will enhance and transform your raw render into a professional work. Some aspects you would need to work with are the following:

- What are render outputs
- Working the render into Photoshop
- Basic corrections
- Working with adjustment layers
- Adding special effects

What are render outputs

Often referred to as render passes, modo's render outputs are extra elements in the render setup that will add a different layer in the final image, depending on the elements we want to work with. In other words, apart from the regular render where you get all the colors, textures, lights, and so on, you can generate many different outputs for a later use in Photoshop during the post-production phase.

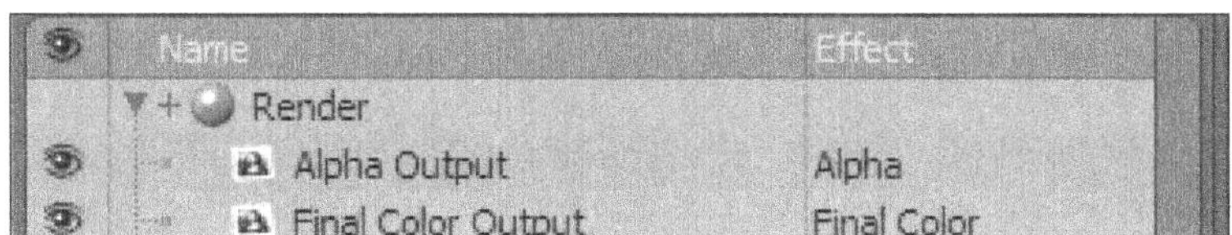

There are many different outputs available to generate, many of them more advanced than others. We will focus on the main outputs, which are more useful for post-production of your image after the final render.

To add an extra render output, you should go to your shader tree. If you expand the render item, you will see first in the list two render outputs. By default, in a fresh new scene, those two outputs are automatically generated. One is the **Alpha Output**, which will generate a black and white version of the image separating the background of the rendered object itself, in case there is actually a background, understanding it as any part of the image that is not the object rendered (useful to use later a custom background for your image, such as a sky) and the other one is the **Final Color Output**, that is the raw rendered image that you will use as the base for the post-production.

From here you can add or change the type of output to suit your needs. If you right-click on the output type in the right column (labeled **Effect**), you will find a vast variety of different outputs to choose from. The other way to create an output is by clicking on the **Add Layer** button, and then navigate to **Special** | **Render Output**. For me, the most quick and practical way to add an output is to duplicate an existing one (right click on > duplicate) and then change its type to the one you need.

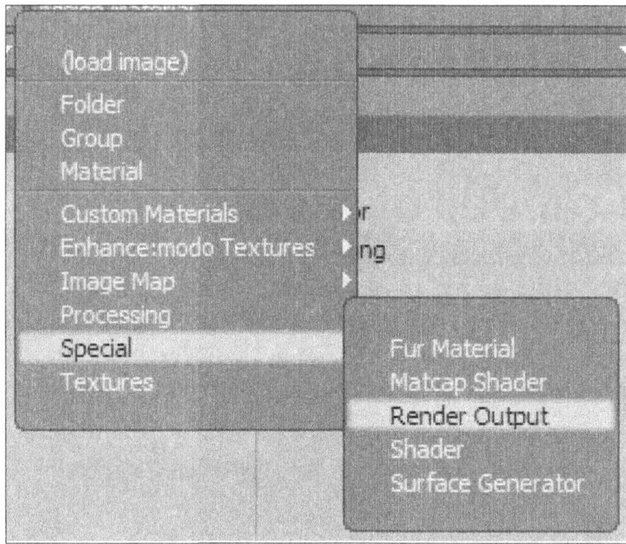

The next thing we will see is the main outputs we will be using in our basic post-production. For that, I have created a pretty random scene as example. Nothing fancy, just some objects from the presets library, an HDRI illumination and a simple white studio background.

So, having this image as the base, we will take an in-depth look at the other outputs we will need.

Isolating materials with the surface ID output

This output will generate an extra layer with the different materials identified with plain color. This will be used later to select easily each material in order to make selective corrections, such as darkening shadows and toning down reflections, only on one object.

You can view the effect of the surface ID output in the viewport directly. If you open the preview window (by pressing *F8*) and change the effect box (top of the preview window) to surface ID you will see the following screen:

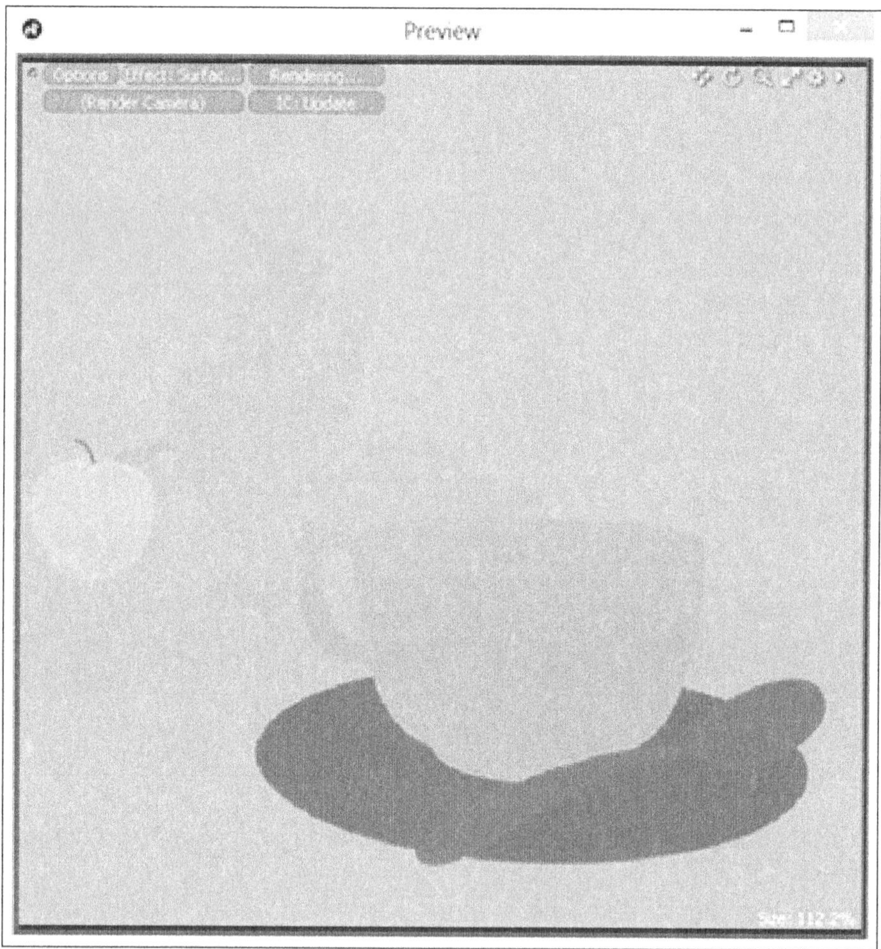

As you can see, every material is automatically assigned to a different random color.

The depth output

This output generates a black and white image (with a shade of greys) that expresses distance from the camera. The areas closest to the camera will be whiter, while the farthest will be darker. When adjusted correctly, the output will look like the following screenshot:

By default, setting the depth output is not always correct—or should I say is never correct—because this is very scene dependent. You should tweak the distance setting to make it look like the previous image; a nice and smooth gradation of greys, with no radical changes to white or black throughout the distance visible.

To adjust the value for the depth output, go to your shader tree, select the output, then in its **Properties** panel, look at the bottom of it for the distance value. That value expresses the farthest visible distance. Tweak the value until you get the smooth look that a depth output should have to work it best.

The ambient occlusion output

Ambient occlusion (**AO**) is an interesting one. No colors, no lights, just occluded light. This output generates shading areas according to contact zones, objects close to each other. If you create an AO output for this scene, the result will look like the following screenshot:

As you can see, the AO shader is independent from the scene setup. No matter how the scene is lit, or the properties of the materials. The AO shader will generate occluded light, or shade areas, defining volumes. This is an essential output that every 3D artist will want to play with.

So, now that we know how each of the basic outputs work and how to create them, we will render the final scene. If you have followed these steps, your shader tree should look like the following screenshot:

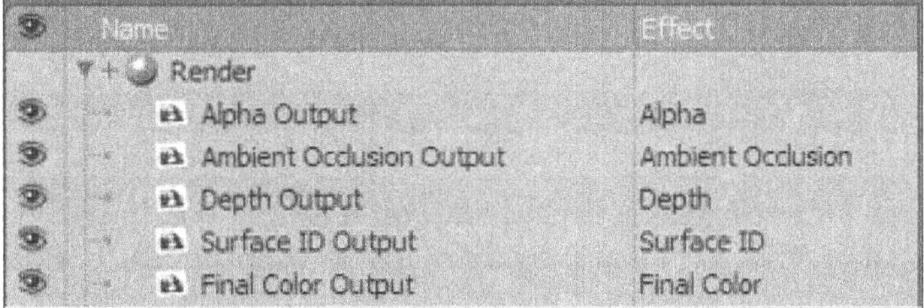

Then we will have the default **Final Color** and **Alpha** outputs, plus a **Surface ID**, **Depth**, and **Ambient Occlusion** outputs. We can now press *F9* to make the final render.

Once the render is completed, you can see any of the outputs by clicking on the **Outputs** button at the top of the render window. You can, from there, select any of the passes to see how it looks.

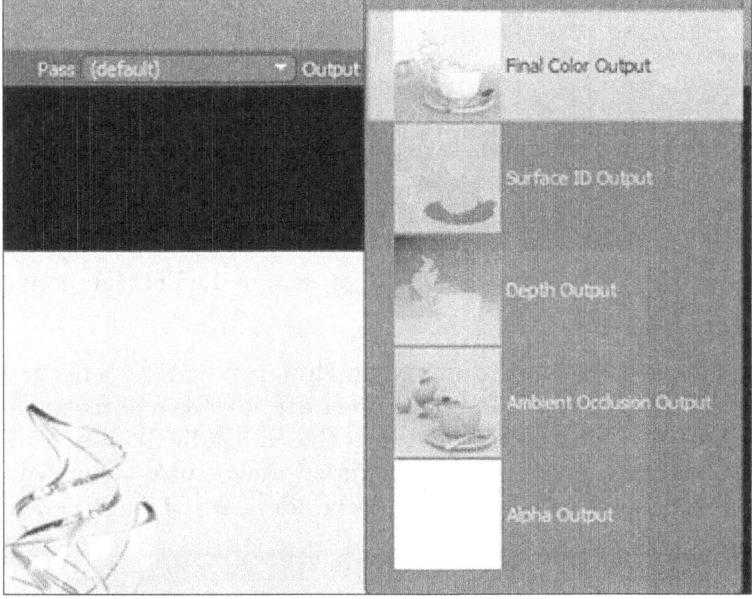

If everything looks correct, go to the bottom of the render window, click and hold the mouse on the **Save Image** button and select the option **Save Layered Image**, that will save a PSD file to load it directly into Photoshop.

Working the render into Photoshop

This section will be covering the core of the post-production phase. It's important that you have at least a basic understanding of Photoshop in order to get the most out of this section.

I will be giving a brief explanation of the main concepts we will be using as we work on the image.

Now that we have our PSD file, we need to open it into Photoshop (by navigating to **File** | **Open**), then take a look at the **Layers** panel (bottom right of the screen).

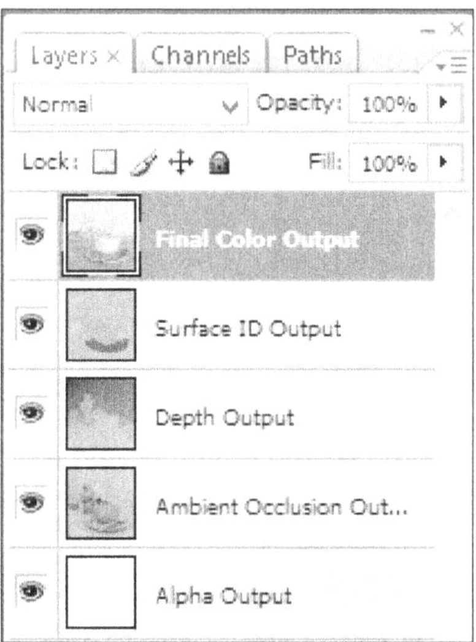

As you see, all the outputs we generated are present in the PSD file, converted to layers.

As a short explanation, layers are different and independent elements of the image, in some way acting like sheets stacked one over the other as real acetate layers. We can make the layers act in different ways over the ones at the bottom using blend modes. We can rearrange them by dragging up or down, make them visible or not by enabling/disabling the little eye checkbox besides each of them, and change their opacity by using the opacity slider.

Blend modes

Blend modes are the way a layer is affecting the other layers that are under it. As usual, there are many different blend modes, but we will focus only on the main ones that we will use in the post-production of our render.

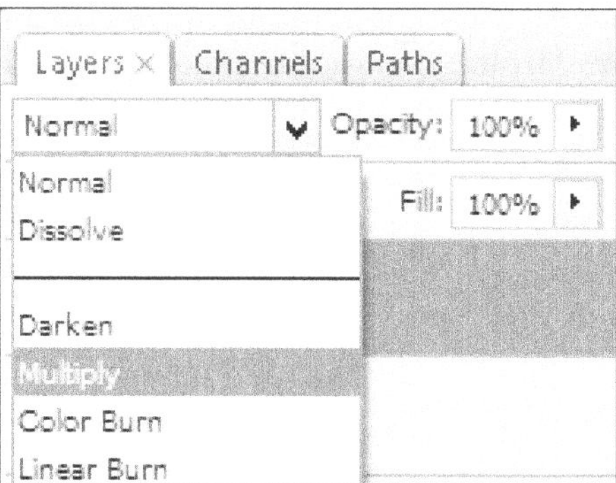

By default, all the layers are set as **Normal** blend mode. Anywhere on the layer that has image information will hide what's beneath it, and areas with partial transparency will allow what's behind to blend through. We will discuss later the different effects we can get with different blend modes, according to each render output.

To change the blend mode of any layer, just select it and click on the drop-down menu at the top of the layers panel, as you see in the previous figure.

Basic corrections

We will start from knowing that a raw render is nowhere near a good balanced image in terms of color or light. The images straight out of modo contain a good amount of information to work with, but they are often washed out or have exaggerated saturation; they require tweaking.

This is normal, no matter how advanced or sophisticated your 3D software is, a raw image should never be used as final art. That's why the post-production phase is so important.

Among other correction, I want to set the four that are the most important to enhance your image for me. As usual, I will specify the route to get to each correction, along with its keyboard shortcut.

Levels

You can find the levels by navigating to **Image** | **Adjustments** | **Levels**; the shortcut for the same is *Ctrl + L*.

Levels are a way to change the light/darkness present in an image. The ideal situation would be an image containing a pure black in its darker areas and a pure white in its whitest. But be careful, this is only theory, and should be interpreted visually independently for each image. Make adjustments to visually enhance your image. Let's study the levels graph a little.

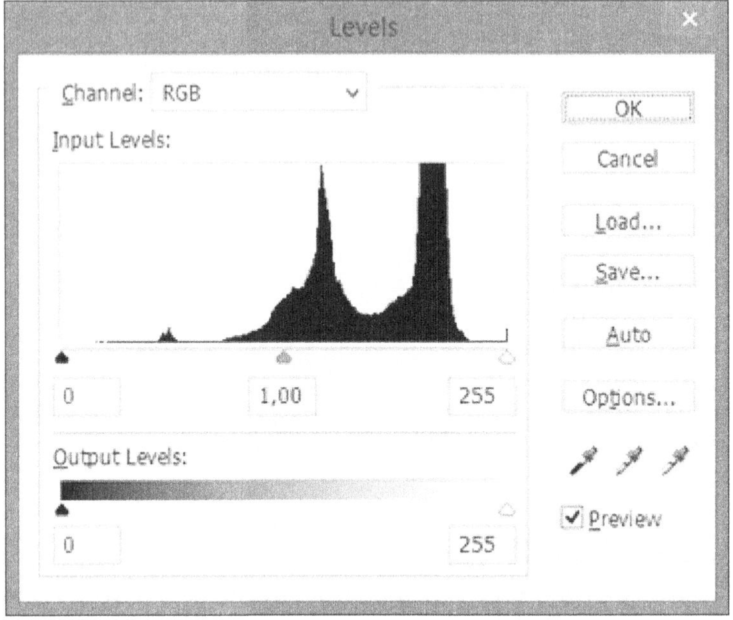

The horizontal value represents the entire gradation from pure black to pure white, with all the shades of grey in between.

In the vertical axis, you will find the amount of pixels in the image for every shade of grey. So how can we interpret this information, and how can we use it to correct our image?

If you check the image again, you will see an empty space at the left of the graph as well as other one at the right. Those spaces mean that the there are no present pixels corresponding to that level of light/darkness, so the image is not covering the full range of greys. That's a regular issue with raw renders, but it's got an easy fix.

There is a slider at the bottom of the graph with three nodes. The left node controls the amount of dark and the right one is for the amount of light. The middle one controls the mid-range greys, half way between pure black and pure white. Move the left node until it meets the beginning of the graph. Do the same with the right node moving it backwards until it meets the finish of the graph. By doing this, you are telling Photoshop where the pure black starts in that particular image, and also which parts of the image are pure white, making it cover the full range of shades. The middle node can be used if the result gets too dark or too light; moving it left or right adjusts the mid-tones. Have a look at the difference in the following screenshot:

As you see, by making the proper adjustments to the levels, the washed out image becomes richer in terms of light/dark. Now the blacks are stronger and the whites are more vivid.

Curves

You can find the curves by navigating to **Image** | **Adjustments** | **Curves**; the shortcut for the same is *Ctrl* + *M*.

This is a tool for controlling light and dark in the image, the same as the levels, but in a more advanced way. You can also manipulate the channels in the image (Red, Green, or Blue) individually, for example, to push more blue in the blacks.

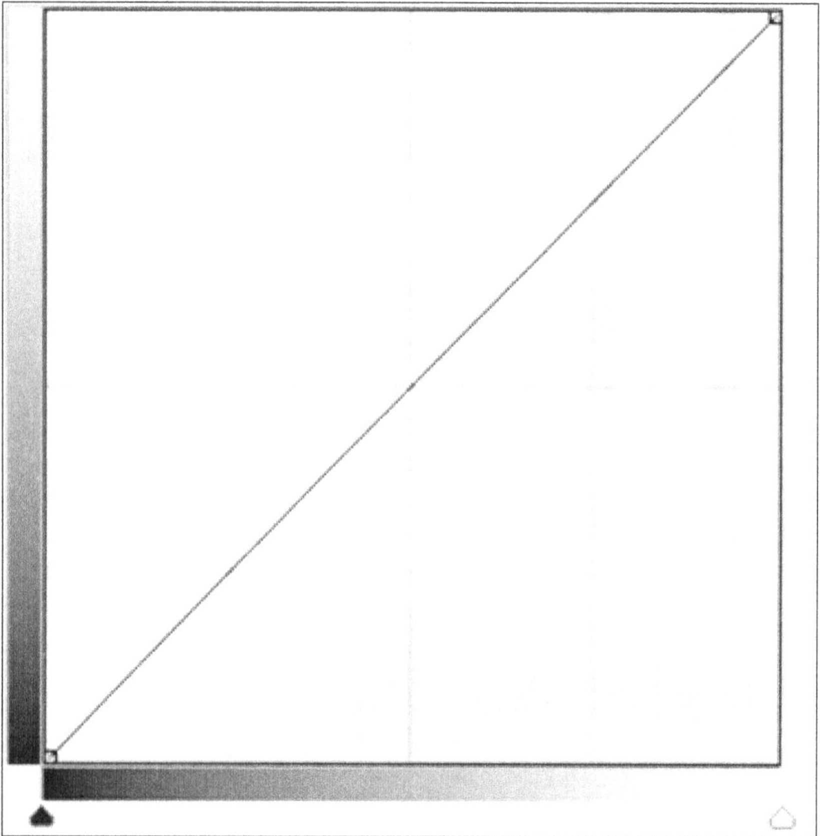

What this does is control darks, mids, and lights independently. So you can make the darks more or less intense, or maybe lower the lighter parts, and so on. It is represented by a diagonal line that goes from blacks to whites. If you click on the line, a node will be created that you can drag to tweak the corresponding part of the image. For example, if you create a node at the bottom of the line, you will be tweaking the blacks when moving it around. A node in the middle will control mid tones, and one at the top will control the lightest parts.

Typically, a good base to fine tune the curve of the image is creating one node in the middle and another in the bottom, and moving down slightly the bottom one, while moving up the middle one, giving the curve an S shape, like in the following figure:

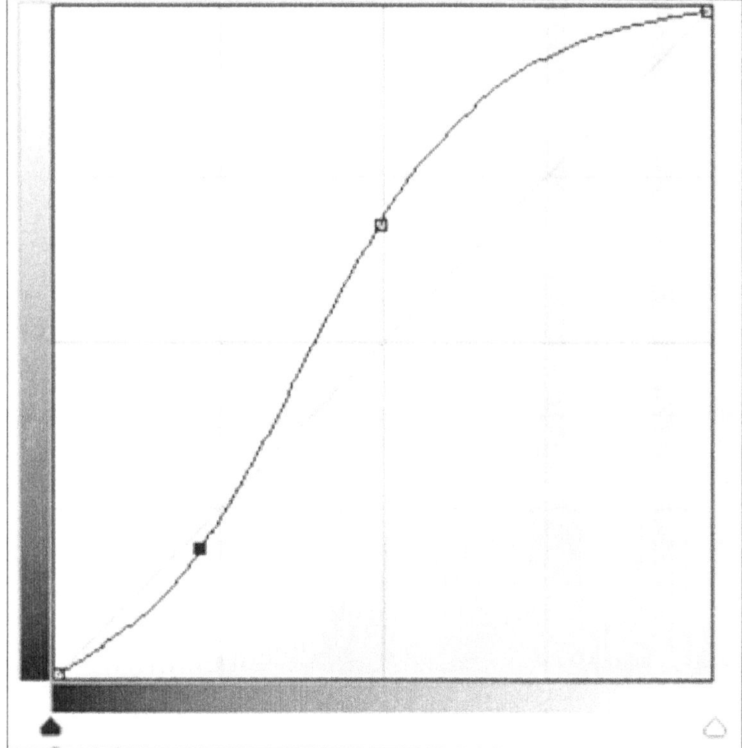

It's easy to read from the previous curve that the procedure was lowering the blacks and raising a bit the mid tones, so we get stronger shadows and dark areas and the mid tones become a bit more vivid. It's the same effect that you get by playing with the levels, but maybe in a more controlled way. Personally, I use both, but it is best to make your own tests to see which one better fits your workflow, or maybe you can use both as I do.

Brightness/contrast

You can change the brightness and contrast by navigating to **Image** | **Adjustments** | **Brightness/Contrast**.

This is a very simple tool. It's pretty self-explanatory: The brightness slider will make the whole image brighter or darker by moving it, and the contrast slider will make the contrast in the image weaker or stronger by adjusting the saturation of the colors.

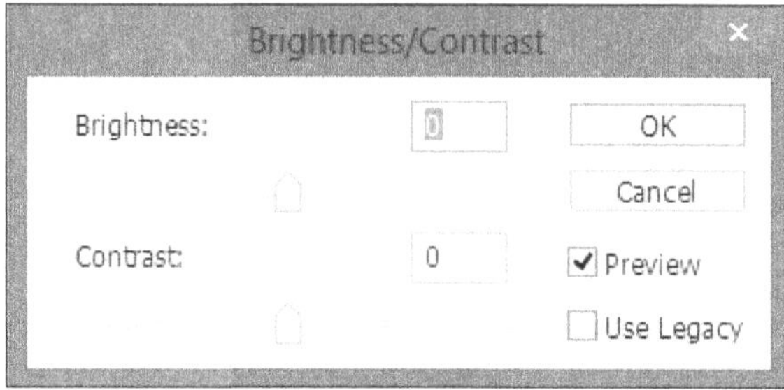

The following screenshot shows a side-by-side comparison of the **Brightness/ Contrast** tool in action for the given image (the left side is the original image and right side is the adjusted version):

Color correction

You can make the color corrections by navigating to **Image** | **Adjustments** | **Color Balance**; the shortcut for the same is *Ctrl* + *B*.

This is a tool for adjusting the general color of the image. You have three sliders for controlling the corresponding balance of every color of the RGB format. So, if you look at the following screenshot, you will see that the more cyan you add, the less red will be in the image. It's about finding a balance.

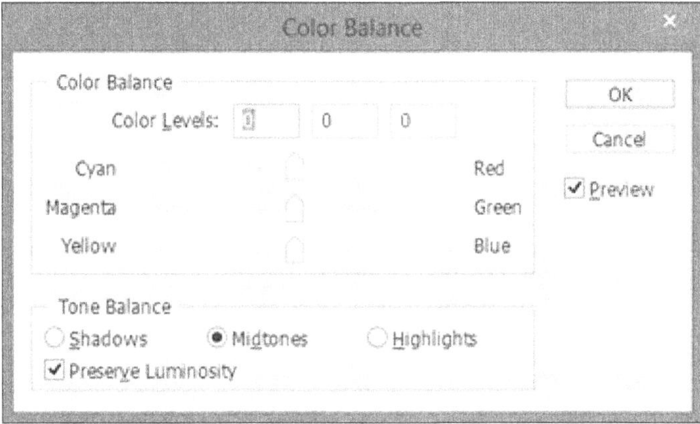

This tool is good for removing a color cast on an image. It can also be helpful to introduce color to neutral images, to change the mood by adding a tint, or when the general color of the image is neutral and you want to get a more cool or warm mood.

Saturation

You can find the change in the saturation by navigating to **Image** | **Adjustments** | **Hue and Saturation**; the shortcut for the same is *Ctrl* + *U*.

This is a kind of variation of the color balance tool, making it simpler and more general. You have a saturation slider in the middle, which controls the general saturation of the image. The slider at the top controls the hue, that is the general coloring of the scene, moving all the color to a warmer or cooler tone.

Finally at the bottom there is a lightness slider that will raise or lower darks, mid tones, and lights all together.

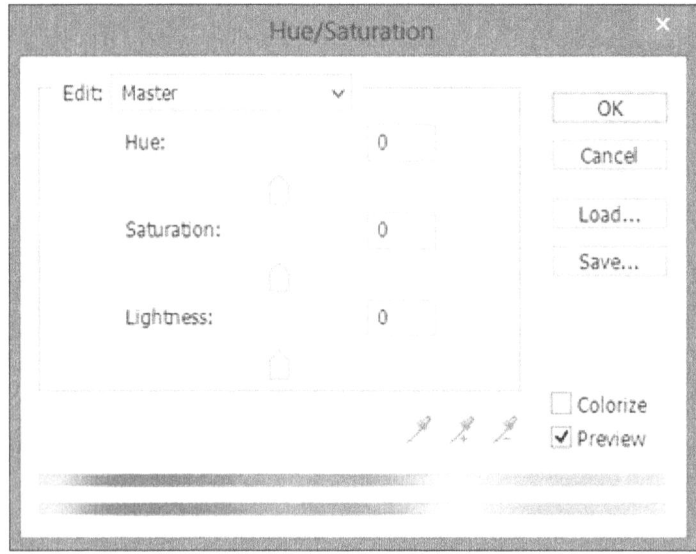

I personally don't find this tool very practical for my workflow, but others do, so it's worth giving it a try. My advice is to use it subtly, since it can make radical changes if you overuse it.

Working with adjustment layers

Until now, while explaining all the different types of corrections in Photoshop, we've been using a simple direct manipulation of the final render where we just make changes and apply it, thus permanently changing the image. This is what we call a destructive working method, meaning that the changes are permanent. And more importantly, if you save and re-open the document, the changes can never be undone, so you only can remove them by undoing (by pressing *Ctrl+Z*).

At this point, we're going to dive into a more professional method by using adjustment layers, a non-destructive method. The benefit of this workflow is that the changes you make to your image can be edited later, always preserving the original image.

So, what is an adjustment layer? Open your Photoshop, load any image, and then look at the bottom of the **Layers** panel. You see the following:

From the many buttons you will see there, I want you to click on the fourth one, looking like a black and white circle. If you put your mouse over that button for a few seconds, you will see a little pop-up help balloon saying **Create new adjustment layer**. Once you click on it, a drop-down menu will appear.

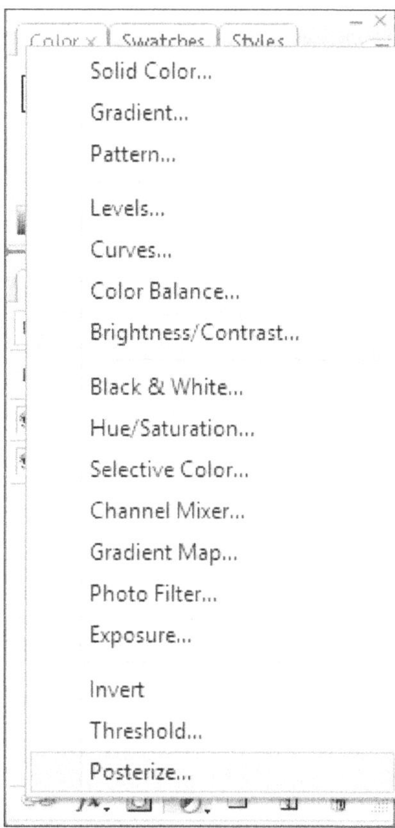

That is a list of the many types of adjustment layers you can create. As an example, click on **Levels**. You will see in the **Layers** panel how a new level adjustment layer has been created.

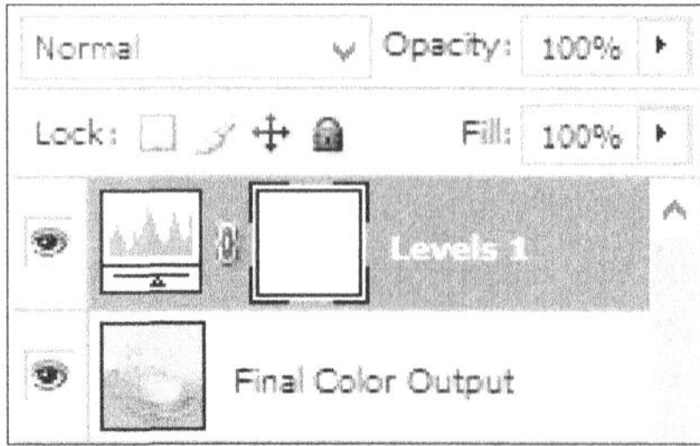

If you double-click on the **Adjustments** layer thumbnail, a new panel will appear, according to the type of layer created. In this case, if you double click on it, the **Levels** tool will appear, letting you tweak the levels as you like.

And then comes the handiness and power of working with the adjustment layers. That layer will affect all the layers under it. It can be disabled and enabled. Its opacity can be changed, so the effect gets more or less intense as you need it. You can change its blend mode as if it were a normal layer, and all in a non-destructive way, always preserving the original image. It is useful for making changes to the image later, if requested by your customer, if you change your mind about something, or you want to create a variation or different version of the image.

Selective enhancing

But there's more about the adjustment layers. You know now that we can affect several layers with it, but, in fact, we can create adjustment layers in a more selective way; for example, apply it to a selection inside a layer. Let's see how it works.

Load any image into Photoshop, then make a selection. For example, I will make a circular selection on a sample windows image:

With the selection done, create a new level's adjustment layer. When created, you will see in the layer miniature, an extra thumbnail showing the shape of the selection I've just made. This indicates that the changes will affect only the selection, leaving the rest of the layer untouched.

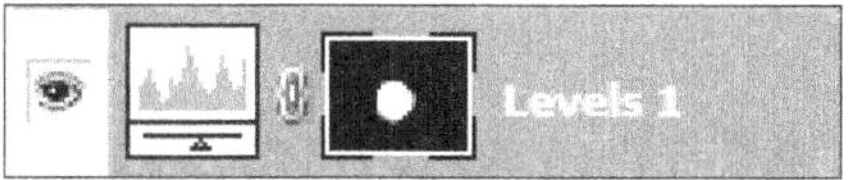

Now you can manipulate the adjustment layer as usual, but you will see how the changes only affect that circular selection. If you change the level for that layer using the adjustment layer, you will see the effect, like in the following screenshot:

Working with adjustment layers applied to selections is a work method I use a lot. This method will let you work with every material of the final render without touching the rest of the image. We will see later, in the *A case study* section how to use this technique to individually enhance each material.

A quick look at the blend modes

Blend modes are the way a layer affects other layers under it. For post-production work, I use just a few of them on a regular basis, depending on what effect I want to achieve or what kind of output I'm working with.

The four blend modes I use for enhancing 3D images are the following:

- **Normal**: This is the default blend mode. It doesn't affect other layers under it.
- **Multiply**: In this mode, the darker areas will darken the layers under it; pure white areas don't effect the areas beneath it. Everything else dims the image beneath it to some degree.

- **Screen**: The opposite to the **Multiply** mode. It brighten the lightest areas, while leaving the dark areas untouched.
- **Overlay**: A mix between **Multiply** and **Screen**. It brightens the lights and darkens the shadows. It's a very strong effect, raising the general contrast.

Adding special effects

Apart from enhancing the image by manipulating the color or light information in it, we can in fact, add elements just by using Photoshop.

Although this kind of "tricks" are not real (as in not calculated by the renderer), we will fake some effects. The benefits for using them are pretty big, because they can be done more quickly than by modo's renderer, and still add to the final image. Let me show you the main post-production special effects that I use.

Bloom (general and selective)

Bloom is a lighting effect that spreads a glow around bright parts of the image. The things like an opened window, or a light bulb can show this effect. You can generate it right inside modo, but it's always interesting knowing how to fake it in Photoshop, in case you prefer the post-production option.

This is a very simple scene, just to show you the effect of the bloom trick. There you see a strong source of light, that is the floating ball. Let's fake some bloom for it.

What we'll do is put a white area over the ball and then convert it into light. You can generate that splotch in many ways such as by making a circular selection or by using the brush tool; it doesn't really matter. The important thing is to have a white area.

Create a new layer on top of the original, and then create a pure white area or selection that covers the ball. I used the brush tool for that, getting the following result:

Remember not to have your white area in the same layer as the image, always in a different one on top of it.

Now, to make it look like we need, we'll just blur it. Navigate to **Filter** | **Blur** | **Gaussian blur** and apply the amount of blur until you get something like the following screenshot:

After you blur your white area, it will look like the previous screenshot. You can now adjust the intensity of the bloom by changing the opacity of its layer. The good point is that it is a non-destructive effect. You can disable or enable it back whenever you want, or change its intensity at any moment. This is a selective bloom (affecting only part of the image).

Instead of making a selective bloom, we can make a general one, affecting the whole image. In case there will be a general light dispersion effect, kind of a "dreamy mood", do the following:

- Duplicate the layer (by navigating to **Layer** | **Duplicate Layer**)
- Apply some blur to the top layer (by navigating to **Filter** | **Blur** | **Gaussian Blur**)
- Change its blend mode to **Screen**
- Adjust intensity with the opacity slider.

Let me show the effect with the help of the following screenshot:

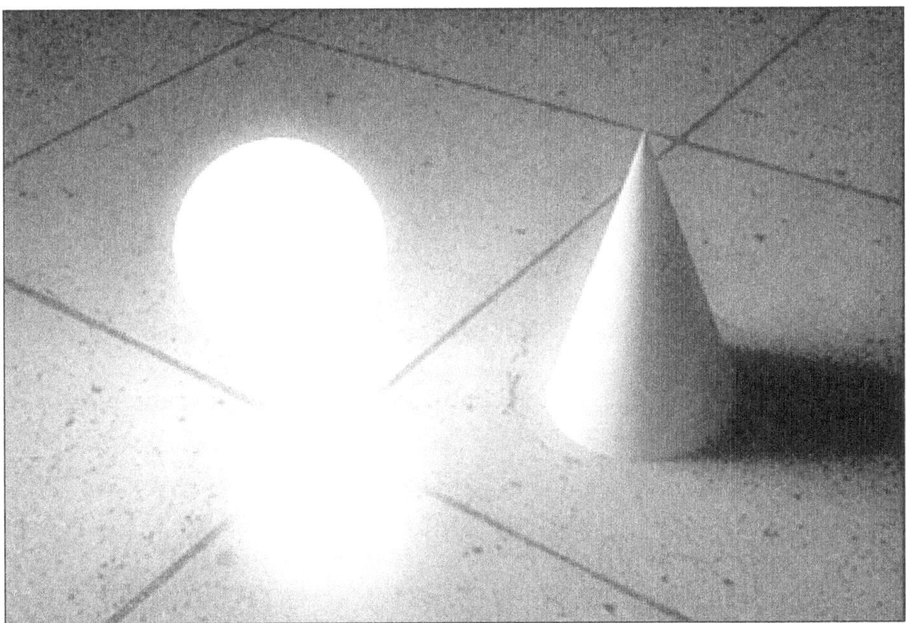

There you can see the light dispersion effect to get a pretty pleasant mood in the image. Used wisely and subtly, this can really enhance your image.

The bleach bypass

The bleach bypass, also known as **silver retention**, is a photographic effect that adds a strong contrast and desaturation to your images, giving a cool cinematic look. I don't really recommend this for your 3D scenes, specially if the shot will be shown to a customer. It's an effect worth knowing, however, because there will be times when you can use it as an eye-catcher. In my opinion it is too dramatic to use it commercially, but don't discard it.

Take a look at the after/before comparison I've made in this picture from `www.worldofstock.com`.

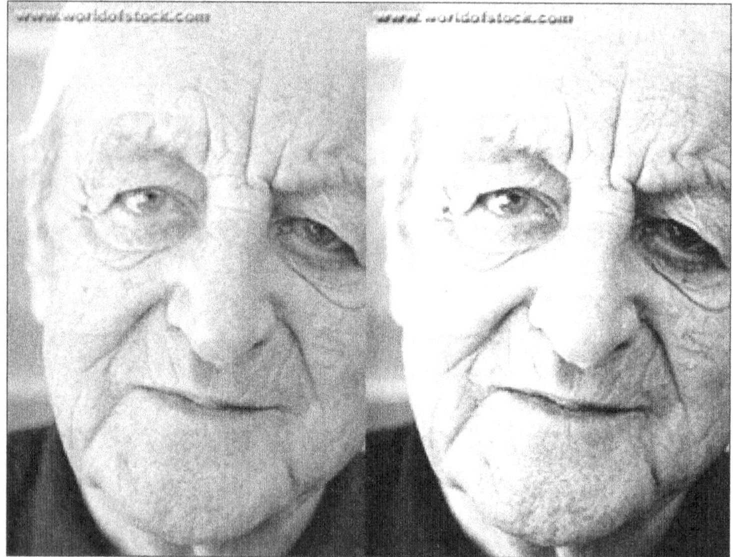

That's the effect of bleach bypass: high contrast plus slight desaturation.
To get this effect, do the following:

- Duplicate the layer (by navigating to **Layer** | **Duplicate Layer**)
- Desaturate it completely (by navigating to **Image** | **Adjustments** | **Desaturate**)
- Change its blend mode to **Overlay**
- Adjust the intensity of the effect with the opacity slider.

Maybe this can work for your scenes or maybe not. It's a very dramatic effect, and not everyone likes it, but some people do, so it's up to you if you want to use it. As always, this effect is non-destructive, so if you want to get rid of it, just disable its layer and it's gone.

Depth of field

We've covered the depth of field in the previous chapters, but we will see now how to fake it into Photoshop, getting a more controlled effect. This method is a bit more complicated since it involves alpha channels.

In order to use this effect, we will need the depth output from the render. If you load the PSD file into Photoshop, you will see the output in the **Layers** panel. First of all, we must move it to the **Channels** panel.

Select the layer corresponding to the depth output. Now select the whole image (*Ctrl+A*) and copy it to the clipboard (*Ctrl+C*). Now, if you look at the top of the layers panel you will see some tabs; change to the **Channels** tab.

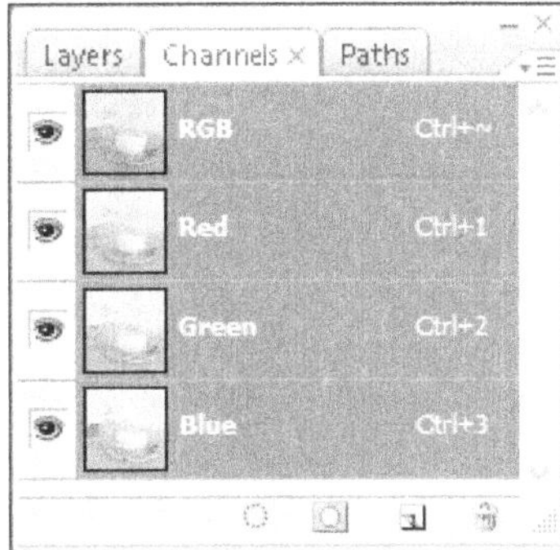

This section of the layers panel contains information relative to the colors channels. Typically, an image contains information of the reds, greens, and blues because they're "encoded" into an RGB format. Apart from that, we will generate a new channel to place our depth output in. Create a new channel by clicking on the third button at the bottom of the panel, labeled as **Create New Channel**. The new one will appear named **Alpha**. Paste the depth output (*Ctrl+V*).

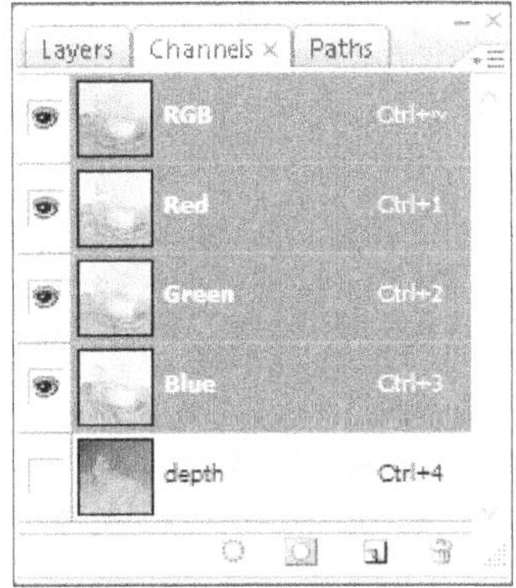

The new channel is automatically named as **Alpha 1**, but you can rename it to your liking by double-clickingon its name. I renamed mine to `depth`. Select the main RGB channel again to continue working normally and switch to the **Layers** tab.

Now the image contains the proper information to apply some depth of field. Go to **Filter** | **Blur** | **Lens Blur** to enter the depth of field tool.

This is the tool to fake depth of field in Photoshop. The only thing we need to set up is the source of information (distance from camera) that we've just created, so we will change the field **Source** to the channel where the depth output is (if it was not already selected).

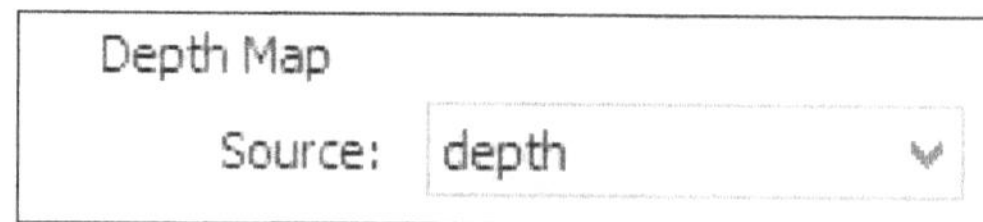

The second thing is adjusting the intensity of the blur. You can set it by using the slider named **Radius**; the higher the number, the stronger the intensity.

Once the source and intensity have been established, you only need to specify the focal point for the image. To do so, just click on the area of the image showed in the viewport of the tool that you want to stay in focus. A blur effect will be applied to the rest of the image based on the distance from camera, so the farther (or closer) an area is in relation to the focal point, the more blurry it will become.

As an example, I chose to have the cup of coffee in focus, leaving the rest blurred. Notice the effect in the following screenshot:

This effect works well when used subtly. If you aim for a more dramatic depth of field, I strongly recommend to using the built-in DOF of modo's renderer. This trick has its limitations, but most of the time, it will be good to use. If you can't wait for a longer render time caused by using modo's DOF, then fake it in Photoshop; but if the render time is not a problem for you, let the render engine do it.

Vignetting

This one is another effect that can give your image an extra touch. Some may like it, some may not, so it is a very personal decision whether to you use it or not.

Vignetting is the effect in pictures taken mostly in low light conditions, where there appears a subtle "tunnel effect", making the corners of the image darker. We can easily fake this effect by the following steps (we will use the previous image):

1. Create a new layer and fill it with a pure white color. Use the bucket tool (G).
2. Now go to **Filter | Distort | Lens Correction**. There you will see the vignette control. You can use its slider to add more intensity to the effect.

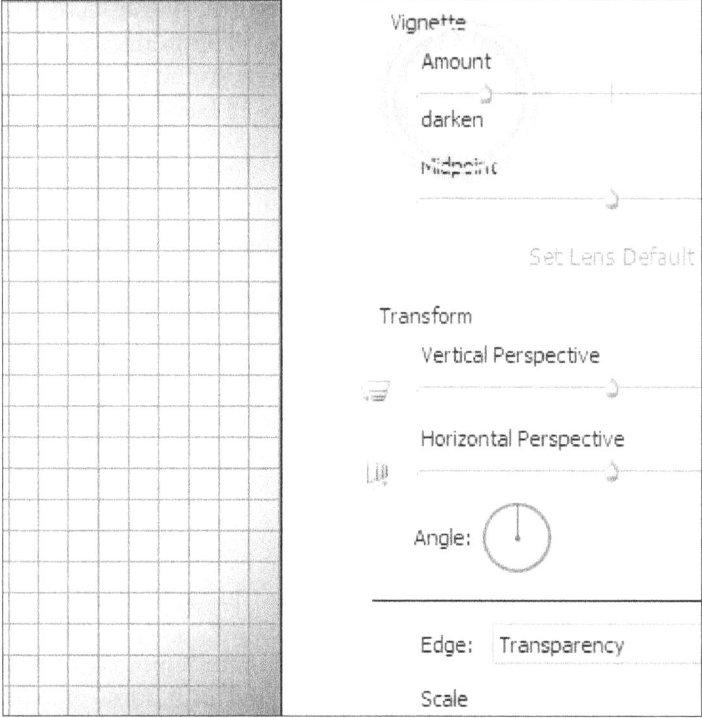

3. Apply the effect and go back to the image.
4. Now if you change the blend mode of the vignetting layer to multiply, the effect will appear. As usual, you can control the intensity with the opacity slider.

The following figure shows the result:

The top image shows the original state, while the bottom one shows the effect. By having the two images together, you can check the difference. The effect is subtle, as I said, but looks very nice, giving it a cool photographic look.

Noise

Typically, for 3D artists like us, the main task related to noise is getting rid of it. But I want to go in the opposite direction: adding noise to our render.

In the real world, noise is always present in photography, with more or less intensity. You will not see photography being absolutely noise-free most of the time (although they can be, depending on lighting and other conditions). Therefore, noise can be in fact what really "sells" the image in some cases. Of course I'm talking about adding a reasonable amount of noise, depending on the supposed light conditions we'll want to mimic. Always remember, low light conditions generate more noise. Don't go for a noisy image of a sunny exterior.

To add noise to your image, go to **Filter** | **Noise** | **Add Noise**. Go for a very subtle amount of it. Let me show you some examples with different values:

The values from left to right are 0.1, 5, and 10. I would recommend very low values of about 2 to 3, or even lower.

A case study

At this point, we should know a lot of tricks and effects to get the most out of our final render. In summary, it is a good idea to take the base image we've been working on and try to enhance it, deciding which effects can be used to make the image pop.

I will show you the step-by-step process according to my personal tastes. You are free to use or not any specific effect, so let's see how far we can go.

First of all, I want to fine tune all the materials in the image, one by one. As I explained earlier in this chapter, I will use the surface ID output to select each material. Using the magic wand, select a material by selecting the colored area that represents it, then create a new adjustment layer from the selection. Repeat this process for each material until you have a layer for all of them.

Then I will make a level's adjustment layer for each. The result is the following screenshot:

Next, I want to use the ambient occlusion output to generate some contact shadows and to enhance the volumes of the objects. I used the AO layer in the multiply mode with a low opacity to get a subtle effect.

To notice the effect, take a look at the following screenshot, where the top picture shows a detail view of the original image, and the bottom one with the AO applied (specially noticeable in the contact area of the glass figure):

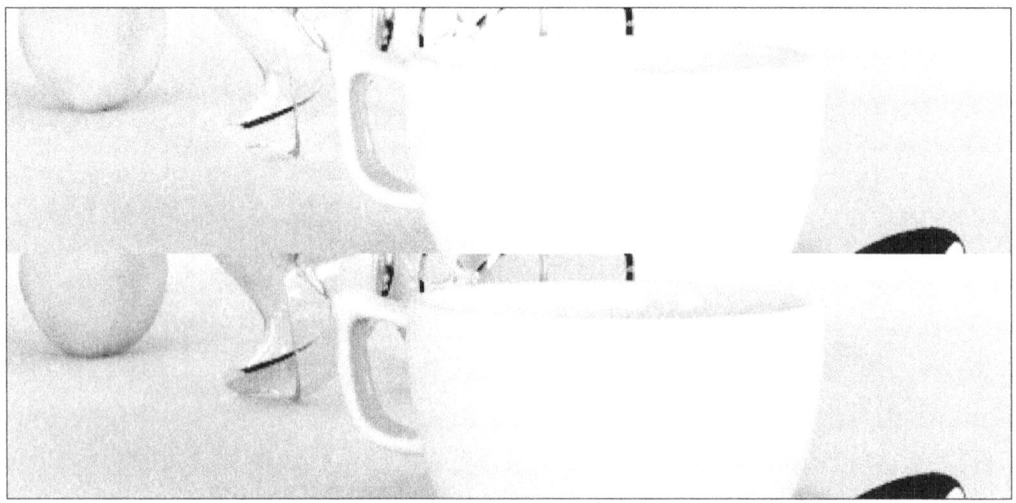

Then I want to add a nice depth of field effect. By placing the depth output in the channels and applying the lens correction, I got the following result:

It's coming along very nicely. Next, I want to add some general bloom, and maybe some selective bloom here and there.

Pretty nice! At this point, maybe I could add some color correction, but I think I will leave the color as it is, since it looks very neutral, and I don't want to see all that porcelain material in a warm tone. Instead, I will add a vignette as my final step.

I would call it done. We could follow the process adding more and more effects, but one important thing on post-production is knowing when to stop. You must keep your mind cool if you want to avoid the risk of producing an overworked image.

Summary

At the end of this final chapter, we have learned how to enhance our original render with many post-production techniques, using different render outputs to add detail to the image as well as many color, tone, or materials corrections.

Also we covered many tricks and tips on how to fake some rendering effects directly in the image, saving render time. You are finally ready to start making your own scene from scratch, modeling your own objects and working along the whole process of getting a good quality image, ready to show in a professional way.

Index

F

G

H

I

K

L

M

N

P

Q

R

S

T

U

V

W

[PACKT] PUBLISHING

Thank you for buying
Building 3D Models with modo 701

About Packt Publishing

Packt, pronounced 'packed', published its first book "*Mastering phpMyAdmin for Effective MySQL Management*" in April 2004 and subsequently continued to specialize in publishing highly focused books on specific technologies and solutions.

Our books and publications share the experiences of your fellow IT professionals in adapting and customizing today's systems, applications, and frameworks. Our solution based books give you the knowledge and power to customize the software and technologies you're using to get the job done. Packt books are more specific and less general than the IT books you have seen in the past. Our unique business model allows us to bring you more focused information, giving you more of what you need to know, and less of what you don't.

Packt is a modern, yet unique publishing company, which focuses on producing quality, cutting-edge books for communities of developers, administrators, and newbies alike. For more information, please visit our website: `www.packtpub.com`.

Writing for Packt

We welcome all inquiries from people who are interested in authoring. Book proposals should be sent to `author@packtpub.com`. If your book idea is still at an early stage and you would like to discuss it first before writing a formal book proposal, contact us; one of our commissioning editors will get in touch with you.

We're not just looking for published authors; if you have strong technical skills but no writing experience, our experienced editors can help you develop a writing career, or simply get some additional reward for your expertise.

OGRE 3D 1.7 Application Development Cookbook

ISBN: 978-1-849514-56-9 Paperback: 306 pages

Over 50 recipes to provide world-class 3D graphics solutions with OGRE 3D

1. Dive into the advanced features of OGRE 3D such as scene querying and visibility analysis
2. Give stunning effects to your application through suitable use of lights, special effects, and views
3. Surf through the full spectrum of OGRE 3D animation methods and insert flashy multimedia

---

Blender 3D Basics Beginner's Guide

ISBN: 978-1-849516-90-7 Paperback: 468 pages

The complete novice's guide to 3D modeling and animation

1. The best starter guide for complete newcomers to 3D modeling and animation
2. Easier learning curve than any other book on Blender
3. You will learn all the important foundation skills ready to apply to any 3D software

Please check **www.PacktPub.com** for information on our titles

Lightning Source UK Ltd.
Milton Keynes UK
UKOW07f1812140415

249642UK00004B/117/P

9 781849 692465